Curvy
and
Loving
it

BY TRISHA PAYTAS

Printed in the United States of America.

ISBN: 1497522803
ISBN 13: 9781497522800

CHAPTER 1

Fat and Fabulous

Okay, so before we go any further, know this. If you're reading this book, you're probably not a size 0, but that doesn't mean that you're fat. Even if you are overweight, society tries to tell you that you're ugly; you're not. I am writing this book for girls whom society deems ugly or unattractive just because we don't look like the photoshopped models on the cover of magazines or the twigs that we see on television. Those are unrealistic views of the real woman and, to be honest, unrealistic views of what the general population finds attractive. I'm a proud size 14 as of the date I'm writing this (I've been a proud size 8 and a proud size 18, for the record), and let me tell you that I have never had a problem getting a man. Why? Because of a little thing called confidence (and a lot of thing called booty and boobies).

I digress. Knowing that you're fabulous is the first step to loving your body and ultimately to loving yourself. The number one question I get asked is: "Trish, how do you have so much confidence?" At first, I get a little offended by such questions. Why do you think I would lack confidence? Is it because I'm a bigger girl? Probably. I think it's so silly: when big girls wear bikinis, they are considered a role model because they are comfortable enough to show their bodies. It's such a sad thing. If a skinny girl wears a bikini, it's no big deal, but when a bigger girl does it, she's brave or making a statement. Total bullshit. Anyway, confidence is key, and in this world, confidence for the bigger girl can be hard to find. This is my secret: I look in the mirror every single day and find something that I love about myself. I started doing this when I was fourteen years old. I would look in the mirror and not like what I saw, but I would tell myself that I did. If you say it enough, you start to believe it. It took me a year to see this self-affirmation pay off, and pretty soon others became jealous of how comfortable I was with my body.

All throughout middle school, I was the "fat" girl. Even though I was about 130 pounds and was by no means the physically largest female in my grade, I was an easy target. I had nice clothes, and I got to visit my dad in California every holiday; there was a lot to be jealous of. That's another thing you should know. All forms of hate come from a deep-rooted issue that has nothing to do with you. Not all haters are jealous (though most of them are), but also, haters see something in you that they wish they could have. I think the material things I was blessed with were the first things to hate at such a young age, so they went for the low blow: the "fat attack." The fat attack is something that is easy for anyone to spew to make him or her feel better about himself or herself. Even if you're slightly out of shape or have a little belly, that'll be the first thing people will throw at you to try to bring you down "fat." I've dealt with this for literally the past fifteen years of my life, so this is nothing new to me. But if you are hearing this word thrown at you or used behind your back, it's because it's the lazy person's way of making himself or herself feel better in his or her own life. I've noticed that a lot of times, physically unattractive or out of shape people themselves will use this word; isn't that crazy? I always like it when people who are not attractive by society's standards will call me fat. In my head I always think, *I can lose thirty pounds and be acceptable to society; you can't lose ugly out your face, girl.* But alas, I don't say this because the number-one rule of being fat and fabulous is to never dull someone else's light so that you can shine. You are going to shine on your own, and you will love yourself so much that trying to hurt others won't be a priority or even a thought that enters your mind.

When I shot *Millionaire Matchmaker* on Bravo, Patti looked at my head shot and then at me and said, "Who is this girl?" I said, "That's me," in my very upbeat tone, to which she replied, "Twenty pounds ago." It was ironic because 1) that picture was taken just one month prior to the show, and 2) because she was no skinny-minny herself. A lot of people asked why I didn't lash back at Patti and her two little stumpy minions next to her, making fun of my weight, and it was because I didn't feel the need to. I was watching this woman with no discernable talent and two other people next to her so desperate for attention slam me for ratings or whatever, and I was okay with that because I knew that I was the one getting the ratings. I was the one that people were going to remember—and I was. To this day, so many people come up to me about that show. They said that I was adorable or sweet; meanwhile, Patti will always be known as the bitch. Who comes out smelling sweeter in the end?

Being fat and fabulous also means that you need to take care of yourself. Let's face it, confidence can come from being a good person and a caring individual, but outer appearance is what we're being judged on. Find clothes that make you feel comfortable. I love wearing tight dresses that show off my boobs and butt; that's what makes me feel comfortable and confident. A lot of bigger girls are afraid to wear minidresses or tight clothing, but its very empowering, let me tell you. Once you walk out into the world showing your tummy without the Spanx, it's liberating. Once you accept your flaws and own them, no one can ever use them against you. If I say that I'm fat and fabulous, the derogatory word of *fat* has immediately lost its context. I own the fact that I'm not a twig, and I own the way I look. I think that makes a lot of people uncomfortable and upset because they haven't figured out yet how to love what they are working with. Aside from just the clothes, treat yourself to a salon day—put extra money aside to get your nails or toes done. I find that pampering myself at least once a month makes all the difference in the world. The running theme of this book will most definitely be: make yourself happy first. As Rick Nelson once sang, "You can't please every-one, so you got to please yourself." And to quote the one and only Rupaul: "If you can't love yourself, how in the hell are you gonna love anybody else?"

It's the truth. If you are not happy with yourself, all other aspects of your life are going to suffer as well. I could tell when I would start losing my confidence;: insecurities would come out in my relationships. I would always think that I wasn't skinny enough or that I would be cheated on because I wasn't pretty enough. All these thoughts would mess with my head, and I would sabotage relationships, thinking that I wasn't wor-thy of someone's love. The truth of the matter was that I didn't think I was worthy of someone else loving me because I didn't love myself.

So I would up the daily affirmations. Instead of just look-ing at myself once in the morning and finding one thing that I loved about myself, every time I walked past a window or a mirror in a bathroom, I would tell myself how fierce I was looking or how my squats were paying off. Or if it was an off day looks wise, I would say to myself, *You're alive, Trish; make this day count.* I would start feeling like I had more purpose on this earth than just myself or my intimate relationships. Even if you're still struggling with what exactly you're put on this earth to do, I promise that will work itself out in due time. Be patient. Continue focusing on being the best you, and every-thing else, love, career, etc., will fall into place—I promise you. You have to trust me because I never thought I would be where I am today. It all worked itself out with faith in me. Don't get me wrong. I always knew that I was destined to be fabulous; I just wasn't always clear on how I was meant to execute it. I'm fabulous now because I look fabulous, live fabulously, and most importantly, I feel fabulous and am now in the position to help others find their fabulous.

One of my favorite little Trishisms is to tell people to be a little narcissistic. Sometimes being a narcissist has a negative connotation, but I never understood why. What's wrong with being in love with yourself? You have to be obnoxiously in love with yourself nowadays because the whole world will try to bring you down. If I didn't look at myself and think that I was better than the rest, I would be broken. I know that may sound bad or conceited, but you should think that you're the best human being in the world. If you think this in your head (you don't have to brag about it), the hurtful things that people say won't matter—as much. Words can sting, but whenever somebody calls me "fat," "ugly," "slutty," or "trashy," I laugh, and then I feel bad because I see how terribly insecure those people are. I know that I'm not fat or ugly or slutty or trashy. I was a freaking lingerie model, for crying out loud. I've won parts on *Modern Family* and such that were originally meant for skinny chicks—because of my swag. When I walked into the Eminem music video audition for "We Made You," there were a dozen other overweight blonde chicks, but they all looked sad and frumpy. Only two put in any effort to wear makeup, and the other ones were sitting with their arms folded over their stomachs that they were trying to hide (as we all were requested to wear bikinis). I walked in and lip-synched to

"Slim Shady" and shook all my loose skin on my thighs like there was no tomorrow. I loved being in that bikini, but that was a journey as well.

If you put on a bikini right now and don't feel like you could walk out on the beach in it and feel comfortable, that's okay. I felt like that for years. Now I'm not saying to become an exhibitionist like I did, but the first time I was naked on stage when I was a stripper was the first time that I loved my body. The profession of stripping can be insanely degrading, but the attention I received from customers lining up to have my naked body on them was an eye opener. For years, I was told that I was undesirable, that I would never be in a relationship unless I lost weight. It was so odd for me to find men not only lining up to be with me but paying for it. There were a million other size 2 dancers they could've had, but they chose me. I know that it seems silly to say that this was uplifting, but it was. I was able to go out on the beach in a bikini because of just getting naked and just doing it. The long roundabout moral of this story is: just do it. They say that you must face your fears, and if you're scared of what other people may think, you must just go and do that which you think you cannot. It's not as scary as you think. People don't generally snicker at others on a day-to-day basis because we all are busy in our own lives. It's those who don't have lives that cause needless drama. So remember that. The worst thing that could happen? Someone calls you fat. Big whoop. Again, that says more about their own insecurities, and you know, just smile and kill them with kindness. To this day, if people call me fat to my face (which probably hasn't happened in over three years), I thank them for their input, and it leaves them speechless.

I went to this audition three years ago for an independent horror film. The director was unbelievably rude to me. It was for a part as a blonde ditz with big tits. I had to strip down to my bikini—a very vulnerable thing for any actress—and the director said to me, "We wanted big tits, not a matching big belly." I think fifteen-year-old Trish would've been mortified, but I knew that I looked good. I was eating clean and exercising regularly for a few months prior, so I was confident. I simply said, "Thank you for your input on my appearance; I will take that into consideration." The other producers in the room looked at him, and he had no rebuttal. One of the male producers walked me out and apologized. One week later, the director called me, apologized, and offered me the part. I turned it down. Two weeks later he called and asked to take me out to drinks. I declined respectfully. There's power in loving yourself, and there's power in loving others. As I mentioned earlier: you don't have to bring down others to lift yourself up. In fact, bringing down others will bring you down.

When I was a teenager and would fight with my sister, we would do low blows at each other's looks. I'm telling you: I never felt worse than I did after picking on something I knew my sister had insecurities about. It would eat at me. The same thing was true with cheating boyfriends: I would get so mad and call them names that I knew affected them—"old" or "has been." I would get so nasty and hurt them, but I was the one who would suffer for weeks because it hurt me that I could be so ugly. It's not an attractive quality in anybody—believe me.

Leaving random comments on people's Instagram or other social media sites (whether you know them or not), saying you don't like their outfit, or that you think they look fat isn't helping anyone. Are you getting anything out of it? No. Are they benefitting from that? No. People think that just because they put something out there to the world, it's okay for them to say whatever they want—absolutely not. If no one is asking for your opinion, you don't give it. Just because you are entitled to an opinion doesn't mean that you are entitled to share it with the world. If it's not helping anybody, don't say anything. You want to contribute something positive to this world. We have a short life; there is no point wasting one precious minute of it on trying to bring drama onto some- one else's life. I don't like Kim Kardashian, for instance. I was never a fan of hers. But there is no way you'd catch me on Twitter or Instagram, bashing her appearance or lifestyle choices. I have way more important things to do with my life than obsess over why she has more money than I do or why she has more fans than I do. None of that helps me or her. I'd be wasting valuable energy hating on her that I could be using trying to better my situation. Instead of saying, "Why does she get everything?" I focus it on me: How do I achieve my personal success? It's a much healthier mind-set and way more productive in accomplishing goals.

Being fat and fabulous is more than just preaching it; it's about doing it. The only way that things change is by people who refuse to go along with the status quo. Fat shaming needs to stop. Don't ever let your fat get in the way of your fabulous.

I used to let weight hold me back all the time; it was always my excuse. I would say, "Maybe I'll get head shots and try acting when I lose a few more pounds," or "I'll try modeling if I can be a size 4 first." Even in everyday life, I'll buy jeans that are 2 sizes too small because I'm hoping to be there one day. Hoping, waiting, anticipating—you're letting life pass you by. I still have jeans with tags on them from ten years ago, hoping they'll fit. Now they're out of trend, and I'm out two hundred dollars. If I were to sit around and wait for weight to come off, I'd be waiting for a while. Look, I'm not lazy; if I want something done, it will be done. If I wanted to be a size 0, I would be a size 0—best believe. But I like the way I feel in my body; I feel womanly. I like the attention I get from the opposite sex; men are in no shortage around me. I take care of my body by exercising, and I reward it with cake. I don't deprive myself of carbs. Life is too short—eat the carbs. It makes me happy. I get asked a lot how am I always so happy, because I can eat McDonald's french fries and not feel guilty for it, that's why. I get the extra butter on my popcorn at the movies, and really, does it get any better than that? Food makes me happy, and if you have a problem with that, you can fuck off.

Why are people so offended by other people's bodies and diets? This is a question I don't think I'll ever know the answer to. It makes no sense. Fitness snobs try to give me unsolicited weight loss advice. Bitch, what makes you think I need your help or want your help? I look at some of these people giving me advice, and I want to tell them, "Go fix yourself up first, and then come back to me." If I see someone with a crooked

10

nose or someone who wears no makeup, is it okay for me to go up and give them the name of a plastic surgeon or offer them a makeover? No. It's not my place. So why do fitness snobs feel the need to do this to people who don't seek their advice in the first place. For these people, you've just got to use the kill-'em-with-kindness technique. Smile and be polite and then strut your fat ass as far away from them as possible. Maybe they'll feel better about themselves, thinking that they are doing a public service for you. If that's the case, you did a good thing by feeding into their ego of being fit and fabulous, if that's what they're going for.

Fat and fabulous is a lifestyle. I say *fat* because it's a word that is just thrown around loosely nowadays. I say *fat* because it's taking away the negative connotation and power of the word. I don't mean it literally, so please don't take it that way. I don't see myself as fat at all; I see myself as healthy. Society may want us to be a one-size-fits-all kind of world, but I'm above society, and so are you. Yeah, you can try to be a size 0 if you want to fit in, but it's so much more fun to stand out. You're big and beautiful. Your perfect imperfections make you unique. I love being different because that means there's no one else in the world like me. I love myself, and that's reason enough for me to get up in the morning. I can't wait for the next day and what it will bring. The possibilities in this life are endless, and opportunities are always knocking at the door, just don't let anything in this world keep you from answering it. You're fat and fabulous, and if the world doesn't like it, tell them to kiss your ass.

Are you motivated yet? Inspired? Heck, I know that I removed all my clothes and typed this, naked, from my deck; that's how amazing I feel. I can't believe how hot I am. I can't believe how soft my body is. I can't believe how amazing this donut is with my morning coffee. Let's keep going, yeah?

CHAPTER 2

Start Today

❦

L ook, it's okay to want to change. Being a plus-size gal my whole life meant also being on a diet my whole life. My body is just one of those bodies that retains all sugars and holds it in my belly, so if I don't watch it, I will balloon up in weight, and I don't like myself to be unhealthy. So I do have to monitor what I eat at times; I can't indulge in everything I want all the time. I have to go for walks. I don't like the gym, but I find alternatives to make sure that I move every day. Sex. I like sex but when I'm not in a relationship, I go and do erotic dance classes down the street. It's all female, and it releases both my sexual frustrations and also gets my body sweating and releasing nasty toxins. I also drink only water and ice teas when going out to eat. It's an easy way for me to cut calories and sugars. I'd rather eat my calories than drink them anyhow. When I go to the movies, I'll have a soda or get the occasional frilly Starbucks drink, but it's not part of my daily routine like it has been in the past.

Maybe this is throwing you for a loop—like, "Trish, you just said you were eating a donut?" Well yeah, if I'm craving one, I'll have it—but not every day.

The point is, to want to change and better ourselves is something that we all do or should be doing. Changing means you're growing, and bettering yourself means bettering the world. We should always strive to be better versions of ourselves. Having said that, the "start today" means don't put your goals off till you become better. Think about it: you're probably better off now than you were a few years ago, and it's because you did that. You got yourself to this new place—this new space. You bought this book because you probably wanted to find ways to love yourself, and that initial step in seeking out help already shows that you're worth so much more than you think. None of us are here by accident; we are all meant to live extraordinary lives.

I mentioned earlier about losing weight to get into acting or modeling. I always thought that to book the roles I wanted to book I had to be skinny, and I wasn't wrong. For years, I had to go to auditions or through agents who told me to come back when I lost weight. As disheartening as it was, I would lose weight, and guess what? I still wasn't skinny enough. I decided to focus on my job at the time, stripping for money, and it wasn't what I loved, so I decided to get back on it. My first professional paying job ever on TV was *The Greg Behrendt Show*, when I was just eighteen years old. I initially went on the show to get a "makeunder" because my look was too over the top, and I needed it to tone down (I submitted myself for this show and talked my brother and dad to coming on with me to give me the surprise "makeunder"). They took out my extensions, covered me up in a long dress with low heels and hardly any makeup. I didn't look ugly, but it wasn't me. They ended up asking me back to be on with a follow-up, and what did I discover? That it didn't matter what I looked like. They liked Trish for Trish, and Greg had me back on the show five more times before it was cancelled, just being myself. I got to dress how I wanted, and they let me wear all the false lashes my little heart desired. It was refreshing to be accepted for myself and not what I looked like on that show.

That spawned other television opportunities for me, and pretty soon, I found myself with an agent. For years I struggled with this agent, who told me that I'm not skinny enough to be the "hot chick," and that I'm not fat enough to be the "fat loveable sidekick." I was told to pick one route or the other, but I didn't want either. I wanted to go out for any role I wanted. We parted ways, and I started representing myself. The first job I booked on my own was the Eminem video, which had my agent crawling back to me. I found that I worked better alone. From that single video, the lingerie modeling opportunities rolled in. I started with small websites and eventually worked my way up to Pipedream Products, the number-one sex toy company, as the face of their plus-size Fetish Fantasy lingerie line, which is sold in thousands of sex shops nationwide. I'm not model height—I'm five foot three—but they didn't care. They all wanted me because I had confidence. I was excited to wear nipple clamps and latex. Most plus-size models want to hide in moo moos and nighties but not me. Why should I be ashamed of my body? Yes, I made a name for myself in the plus-size modeling world, but that didn't mean that I was going to only pigeonhole myself as the "hot fat chick." I went out for a skinny role that was meant for size 0–2 on *Modern Family*, and I got it! I started my YouTube channel to show that I had star potential. A lot of agencies and production companies didn't want anything to do with me before, but now that I have an audience and a voice, they all want Trish. I get calls and offers daily because they see people responding to what I'm putting out there, and I did it on my terms and waited for no one. If one avenue doesn't work out for me, I have five other paths already lined up to blaze through.

Alas, this isn't about how fabulous I am—oh wait, it kind of is! But it's also about how fabulous you are. Look, if I waited to get skinny or if I waited for others to notice things about me that I already knew, I would not be where I am today, and I would not be writing this book. You've got to go for it, and you can't rely on anyone else but yourself. Set goals for yourself and start working toward them today. Never say that you're not pretty enough, not smart enough, not educated enough, not rich enough, not skinny enough—none of that matters; I promise you. People try to tell you that you can't do something because they can't do it themselves. People try to laugh at your dreams because they're too scared to go after their own. I had a careers class in grade school. In grade five, I told the career counselor that I wanted to work in the entertainment industry. She told me that nobody had that career. Even at ten years old, I knew that people worked in that field. Really? Nobody works in entertainment? How the heck do movies get made, lady? She was a crack job for sure, but to a lot of other 10 year olds who might hear something similar, they might believe it because it's coming from an adult, and they're just a kid.

Kids, don't you hate that too? "Oh, you're just a kid; you don't know." Or people telling you that you're too young to have an opinion, to have a voice, or to make a difference in this world. I don't care what age you are; you are never too young or too old to do anything. Britney Spears was on the Mickey Mouse Club by the time she was a preteen, and Teri Hatcher didn't get her big stardom breakthrough role till she hit forty. We all have our time, and it doesn't matter what age. Size can hold a lot of us back—as can age—but don't let it. Both of these things are superficial bullshit that the world is trying to brainwash us with. But those of us who can break the mold and start changing the way society views us today are the ones who will succeed.

Think about it: those who get glory and fame and riches are those who are pioneers, groundbreakers. The first to come through with something are the ones who are remembered; the followers are just an afterthought. So if there is no one like you in the field that you want to be in or the life that you want to live, then you've got to be that change that you want to see. You've got to be that breakthrough. It's not easy, but it will be worth it.

This moment is all that we have; tomorrow is promised to no one. If you want to get healthier, start today; want to get fit, start today; want to be a star, start today. You have to start somewhere, and you have to start sometime, so why not start today? But through this, remember the first rule to being fat and fabulous: loving yourself. You want to get healthier, great, but that doesn't mean that you can never have a donut. You want to get fit, wonderful; that doesn't mean that you can't be a couch potato every now and again. You want to be a star— shine baby, but you're not going to be the next Marilyn Monroe in a day. Be patient with yourself, and while you're working toward your goals, remember to reward yourself with each step of progress you make. Maybe you finally got those head shots you needed or signed up for acting classes. Don't forget to tell yourself how proud you are. If you took the stairs instead of the elevator at work today, don't forget to take a selfie of your butt to remind you how hot you're looking.

I always want to better myself—tighten myself up. I work out, and people ask, "Why do you work out if you're so happy being fat?" I want to be the best me, and, honey, I'm never going to be skinny. Why? Because I'm curvy and loving it! My curves are me; my curves give me confidence, and they're my inspiration and my badge of honor. I'm in the curves society, and not every girl was blessed with lovely lady lumps. I'll be curvy and loving it for life, so you've just got to start getting used to it, planet earth!

CHAPTER 3

Believe to Achieve

Have you ever heard the saying "fake it till you make it?" Well it applies to self-love as well. A lot of people say that in order to achieve success, you have to appear to have the success you desire already. It's kind of twisted, but it makes sense, and this is exactly how I achieved my overdrive of confidence.

In middle school, when I would get teased about my weight, I thought the solution was to lose weight, and that would fix everything, but that's just not the case. You lose weight, and then people still call you fat or find something else to pick on you for. You lose weight, and then maybe you're not happy with the way you look or feel; your energy may be low, or you may feel like you're neglecting some of the best parts of life. You lose weight in hopes that maybe other people will like you; they won't. So you have to lose weight for yourself or don't do it all. I'll tell you this: even when I was "thinner," people still found things to get on me about. For instance, I would go from a size 12 to a size 4, and then I wasn't "fat," but I was "poor" or "tacky" or "slutty" or "sickly." People who are going to hate on you are going to hate on you because they hate themselves. So if you change what they "hate," they'll find something else to take their insecurities out on. Stop thinking it's about you and what you have to change.

The truth is that I didn't want to change all that much with the way I looked in high school. However, I thought I needed to—to survive or to be accepted by society as a whole. I thought that since I didn't have a boyfriend in high school, it must be because of my weight, which is what everyone would pick on me for. Teenage Trish logic said that I would never have a boyfriend in life if I didn't change. It's the same thing I thought about success: I never was the smartest in school or the richest, so I thought that I had to change in order to make these things happen for me later on in life. As I started to "change" things about me, I started losing who I was; I started losing Trish. One of my favorite teachers told me that I had a spark when I started there, which was my second school, and that he couldn't see it anymore. He would try to coax it out of me—if something was wrong with my home life—but I just didn't know at the time. I would skip meals, which would make me lightheaded; I would try on my sister's jeans, which would make me depressed. Nobody was acknowledging my change, which discouraged me completely. I wasn't focused on what I wanted to do after high school and how I was going to accomplish all my dreams. I was too busy focusing on what people wanted me to be, and that's when I knew that I needed a change.

People saw that I was trying to change and fit in so hard, but they refused to acknowledge my efforts, so I knew I had to fake that I didn't need their approval. For the record, you never need anyone's approval in life. Even in my adult life, so many agents and managers and producers have told me that I'm not going to make it in the entertainment industry because of this or that and the other thing. I didn't need them telling me what I can and can't do. I knew that I was meant to be in the business of performing, and well, it looks like I'm not going anywhere soon. I didn't need their audience; I created my own. But I digress. Back in school, I would start wearing the clothes I liked again. I would wear something crazy, and they would laugh at it or tell me that it looked bad on me. One day I wore this all-silver-sequins jumper to school with a pink shag crop jacket. Everyone laughed at me and told me how ugly it was. They all knew that my dad lived in California, and so I told them that it was given to me by Paris Hilton (not true at all), and instantly, they all changed their tune. Everyone in school was talking about how I knew Paris Hilton, and I remember a few girls wanting to try on the jacket. A few weeks later, I wore the same outfit, and it was stolen out of my gym locker. Again, it was girls just trying to be cruel, but I guess it was fabulous enough that it was worth taking. By making up something so superficial, that outfit went from hideous to most coveted; it just goes to show what beauty really is. It's all in the eye of the beholder, and it's all subjective. Why do you think name brands do so well? One influencer says it's cool, so it's cool. Low-end wholesale stores get bad reps because of propaganda. Fashion, beauty, style are all superficial, so try not to mind that so much. Wear what you love because one day you could be the influencer, and you could actually start a new trend yourself.

As for my body size, girls could only describe me as fat. They'd make fun of me for wearing spandex because the soft shorts they'd wear would ride up in between my thighs because I didn't have that thigh gap. That tune changed in high school when Jennifer Lopez started to become more known for her booty. I had to continue rocking the spandex because I didn't have a choice. My thighs were continuing to grow and didn't want chafing. I'd wear the spandex, and people would say that I had a camel toe (ironically, that's a thing that most adult men find sexy; they love to see the outline of a woman's most sacred and sexual body part). I remember the exact day that I stopped wearing oversized shirts to cover my spandex and wore a tank top to accentuate it. These two girls made vomiting noises as I walked past, and I said, "Jealous you still have the body of a twelve-year-old boy?" Not the most mature thing, but I was a teenager; I was trying to survive. To which one of the girls said "Eww, your butt is so big. Who wants that?" And I replied, "Apparently Ben Affleck doesn't mind"–he was dating Jennifer Lopez at the time. The boys next to them started laughing, and the one girl actually cried–actually cried. Up to that point, I had spent years holding back tears so that people wouldn't see me cry; it was bizarre to be on the other end. I thought that it'd feel good, but it didn't. I realized that I needed to love myself and be confident without bringing others down.

From then on in school, I would still flaunt my style and my figure. However, what bothered girls more was when I didn't react to them. If girls would make pig noises at me, for instance, or bark or oink at me, I would smile and keep walking, and I would strut, baby. I would strut. The strut is sort of my security blanket. When I get scared to go into an audition, walk into a party, go on a first date, the best way for me to believe I'm not scared it is to fake a power walk. By walking into a room and appearing to be confident, you'll attract the right kind of attention. We would have to swim in school for gym like twice a year. We'd all have to walk out in our swimsuits from the locker room to twelve feet to the front of the pool and sit on a bench and wait. All the boys would change the fastest, and they'd sit on the bench and watch all the girls walk out. Most girls walked out in clumps, cliques, or pairs. I didn't have a clump, clique, or pair, so I would walk out alone. From about grade five through grade seven, I would try to cover my boobs or stomach. I would walk really fast and avoid eye contact. After junior high, I would still wear a one-piece, but I would stick out my chest and play with my hair. Again, snarky comments would come out, and I would hair flip all day. That's not to say that I wasn't scared or that I was confident with my body at the time, but I pretended to be.

After a while, girls would get bored with trying to bring me down because I wouldn't acknowledge the hurt. I pumped myself up every day: I would tell myself that I'm pretty. I would practice my acceptance speech at the Oscars in my living room. Before I got in the shower, I would pose for the mirror as if I were on a photo shoot. Pretty soon, I wasn't just pretending; I was visualizing all this happening. I was beginning to believe that I was an actress; I was a model; I was destined to achieve my dreams. What started out as something to just get me by turned in to my life credo: that anything I believed I could and would achieve. I'll tell you something: teenage Trish would not believe the life she was going to lead. If I had told myself at fifteen, "Trish, not only are you going to love your body, you're going to flaunt your body. People will pay to photograph that body; companies will hire you to model their lingerie, and other girls will aspire to your body," she would've had less of a struggle.

Girls write to me all the time, saying that they started to love and feel comfortable with their bodies because of me. I'm not saying that they have the same body type as me, but it's more of the overall feeling. You don't have to look like this person to feel good about yourself. You don't have to look like that person to be considered beautiful.

I've attracted so many guys based off confidence alone. I know it sounds cliché to say that "confidence is sexy," but it is. When I walk into any room, I tell myself that I'm the best looking one that's going to be in there. I remind myself of all that I've accomplished. When I was in high school, it would be something along the lines of, "You travel to California three times a year," and that would be enough for me. Now it's, "You've written books; you have your own perfume; you have people who admire you." So it can be large-scale, small-scale—anything, even if it's, "I'm the best pet owner," or "I have the best skin." Find something and own it and say that you are the best; believe you are the best. You don't have to say it out loud or to anyone in particular. They are going to feel that energy; they are going to jump onto that belief, even if they don't know it.

It's okay to think that you are the best. You should think that you are the best because the whole world is going to try to bring you down. You'll find some support along the way, but that'll just be the cherry and sprinkles on top. You have to face the world as if it's you against the world—as if no one else will ever back you up. Breathe for a minute because, like I said, you will have some true blue amigos, but just face the world as if you don't.

By believing that I am the best, it radiates to others. By smiling through pain, by laughing through fear, I'm showing confidence. By not bringing others down, I'm showing positivity and strength. All of this adds up to one sexy woman.

The other day, I was on my morning walk, and this guy who was a Sammy Davis Jr. impersonator pulled his car over to talk to me. I will tell you that this is not uncommon. I would say that on the average, I get about two guys who go out of their way to talk to me on a daily basis. I wrote on my blog last year about a drugstore excursion where I was approached by four different men, all wanting some Trish, and I was looking one heck of a hot mess, let me tell you. Anyway, the look-alike pulled over, and he got out of his car. He asked me my name and said the he liked the way I walked. He said, "I watched you walk for five minutes, and there is just something about the way you walk." I found it interesting if nonetheless unique. Guys may stare at my tits or my eyes or try to focus on my words or tell me that they like my hair, but the walk is what struck me. The way a person walks speaks volumes, really. It's the way a person carries himself or herself that makes him or her attractive. A man with nice broad shoulders and a warm smile is much more appealing than that of someone who is slumped over and expressionless. You want to invite the world into your world. Remember: this is your world; the rest of us are just living in it.

The next time you walk past a window, look at yourself. Look at yourself and tell yourself how sexy you are. Be completely vain with it. Look in the window and take a picture of yourself in it to remind you how sexy you are. I don't look at a picture of myself anymore and see bad things; I only see good. Let's say, for instance, that my stomach is not as tight in a photo. I don't see that; I see how awesome my hair looks or how good that cheesecake was at the lunch I just had before I took that photo. Also, by not stressing about the little things, that stress will actually come off of your appearance as well. I would worry so much about my tummy, and it would bloat me even more. Once I stopped caring, it kind of went away on its own. I wasn't focused on it, and it really worked itself out.

When you're scared, strut. When you have an ugly day, go take a picture in the mirror and look for the hotness. If someone calls you fat, you smile and go eat something that they wish they could eat. Just live for you. What other people think of you is not any of your concern. People are going to talk about you regardless; give them something to really talk about.

It's so funny when people are surprised by my confidence. Why—just because I'm a bigger girl, and I'll wear a bikini? If that's confidence, then so be it. I don't consider it to be this great demonstration of confidence. I consider it just being me now. I just live. If someone wants to applaud me for wearing something they wouldn't, whatever. Love me or hate me; I'm going to do me. You do you. At the end of the day, you're going to bed full or hungry. Are you full and happy on cake or hungry and miserable for any sort of nourishment? Are you full on life or hungry for any kind of happiness? Are you full of love or hungry for attention from others? Self-satisfaction is the easiest way to be happy in this life. To be truly happy is a choice that you can make for yourself, and no one will ever be able to take that away from you. Today is the day to tell yourself how amazing you are, even if you don't believe it right now because one day, I promise you, you will believe it, and so will everyone else.

CHAPTER 4

Be a Narcissist

I take, on average, one hundred selfies a day. I look in the mirror probably ten times that amount, and my house looks like a shrine to myself. I didn't always love how I looked, nor did I always like how I looked in pictures because I didn't look like Britney Spears, Kate Moss, etc. I would avoid mirrors and not put much effort into my appearance. I didn't care about my appearance, and in turn, no one else did either.

Once I started to take a little more pride in my appearance, the teasing would happen a little less, and I liked that. As awful as it may be, this world is superficial and will judge you on your looks. Perhaps you're not the classic beauty, but maybe you're more edgy, unique, or exotic. Find your niche and flaunt it all around. Pretty soon you'll start making people see a different kind of beauty if you don't fit into any of the current "beautiful" categories. The image of beauty is constantly changing. In the years of the Greek gods, women who were large with bellies were considered beautiful because they could afford to eat, and to this day, classic Greek or Roman statues show women with fallen breasts and round thighs and stomachs. In the Renaissance period, women loved having the small waist. This trend carried on for years until the early 1920s. There were even fainting couches to catch the women whose corsets were on too tight for too long, suffering to get what was current at the time as beautiful. In the 1950s, the culture was the curves: Marilyn Monroe, Jayne Mansfield, etc. were size 14, which is the equivalent to the current American dress size of an 8. I started "plus size" modeling at a size 8! Meaning that in America you are considered overweight if you are a size 8–14 and obese if you're anything larger. How crazy is this logic? Heroin-chic was a term in the '90s that cultivated this phenomenon that all women must be under one hundred pounds to be attractive, which really sparked a whole slew of eating disorders and a way of thinking that you have to starve to achieve collarbones and be found attractive by men.

The point is this: beauty is in the eye of the beholder, and the main beholders, unfortunately, are fashion magazines and pop culture media. But guess what? That beholder sucks! As I mentioned earlier, if you embrace who you are and what you look like and take it to the tenfold, people will respond.

When I first started taking selfies on social media in 2006, Myspace was all the rage. I would start by posting pictures of myself in the bathroom mirror every day before school. The more popular I became on Myspace, the more hate I received. I would start feeling the self-conscious old Trish creep in:

voices in my head telling me that I shouldn't be posting. I would get comments like, "kill yourself," "your body makes me never want to eat again," and "who let this beached whale use a computer." Mind you, at the time, I was eighteen; I was a size 6. I wasn't fat, and I had a flat tummy. I just had a booty, some breasts, and a softness to my body. I wasn't tight, but I wasn't flabby either. I would hold back posting pictures as often as I was used to because I couldn't bear to read the comments. I would look at the "Myspace famous" girls who were getting to pose in Playboy and felt bad that I wasn't looking like that. I would post my one picture a week, and I would get a comment like, "Eww...she's still posting pictures? Just stop, you fat cow." It really hurt me—not because she called me fat. At that point, I was over that word, but it was more because she was controlling my life and taking away something that made me happy. Who the hell was this random chick in New Jersey, and was she going to stop me from being happy? What kind of power does that give people? So I started being obnoxious about posting pictures—like every hour in between classes. I was getting more followers and more comments, and the haters were getting hated on by people who supported me. Slowly, haters would either get insecure themselves (because they had their own picture on Myspace), or they would just get bored or too worn out to comment on ten photos of me a day. Showing that I was confident in my posting and not stopping because of mean comments not only gave me power but also gave power to others to do the same. I would start posting pictures in bikinis, and I would get comments like, "Wow.

I've never seen a body like that," or, "That's what a real woman should look like," and this was the first I was seeing something like this on the Internet or at least in the places I was looking. I'm not saying that to be a real woman you have to have curves, tits, and ass—quite the contrary. I think to be a real woman you have to own the real you. If you want a fake nose, you can get it; you're still a real woman. If you're a vegan and only eat raw food, you're a real woman. If you gorge yourself in burgers and fries, you're a real woman. Real women are happy, fat, skinny, healthy, unhealthy, dumb, and smart. If God created you, you're a real woman. So the idea of "real women should be like—" is ridiculous because we're not robots; we are real fucking women.

So I was the picture queen on Myspace, and I wanted to expose more of myself and who I was, not just my body. At the time, YouTube was the only place to upload a video and have an HTML link to share it on your page, so I started uploading random YouTube videos of me telling jokes, rapping, and just everything I enjoyed doing. Now this gave haters a whole new fuel to try to bring me down. At first, I'd delete comments, and sometimes I'd delete whole videos if someone told me I looked fat or something in them, but I had to apply the same mind-set to my videos as I did to my photos. I had to push through the hate. At first, that meant not reading any comments under any circumstances—the good or the bad—but just post because it made me happy and move on. I started getting e-mails from people that I admired in the entertainment industry, telling me that they enjoyed my videos, and that's when I knew it wasn't all hate, and that the hate I was getting was from people who didn't matter. The hate comments would come in the middle of the day when people should be at school or work, but they were at home, smoking pot, unemployed, telling me I was worthless. The validation was nice, and it helped me at the time, but validation from others isn't necessary if you can find it within yourself. Let me explain.

To hear someone you admire in whatever industry you're in praise you is an amazing feeling. It feels good. However, if you put all your worth into what others say about you, it can backfire. If, for instance, you go to an audition and you either a) never hear back from them or b) hear feedback criticizing your talent or appearance, it can really damage you. You'll question if you even belong in that industry or if you'll ever make it. I've had so many casting agents tell me that I'm too fat to be in entertainment. Well guess what, bitches, I'm in entertainment, and it's my full-time job. So what now? Oh, that's right, you're a casting associate who has to have a second job because you're at the bottom of the Hollywood chain. I was already above them by scoring the audition. If they didn't like me, it was fine because I was working my dream job, and they were still paying dues.

You are above other people. I know we are taught that we are all equal, and that no one is above anyone else. Well, let me tell you, that's bullshit. You're above the person who calls you fat. You're above the person who tells you you're worthless or unintelligent or who laughs at your goals and your dreams. You're above anyone who tries to bring you down, and they know that otherwise they wouldn't need to, even on the playing field at their level, which is below you. Some people may consider this narcissistic, but that's okay; be a narcissist. Do you know how many people in this life are going to try to bring you down? I can specifically name one hundred people in my mind who have tried to tell me that I'm not good enough or that I can't do something. I can name one hundred people from my hometown, including guidance counselors, who told me that nobody can have a job and prosper in California. I can name one hundred people who have told me in my adult life that I was silly to think that I could make a career without college. College wasn't for me, and I knew this. I knew that what I wanted in life wasn't going to be helped by college, so I didn't go. Not everyone knows this, and some people need college to achieve their goals, much like I needed social media to achieve mine. Now if that doesn't sound shallow, I don't know what does. But it's true. To build an empire in the world of entertainment, you need an audience, and with social media, you can build your own audience and have people need you rather than you needing them. A few years ago, I wasn't cast on a reality show, and my feedback was that no one cares about my life. Here we are in 2014, with over 750,000 people total across my entire social media board who follow me to keep up with what makeup I'm putting on my face or what outfit I'm wearing or what my opinions are on current events! Now TV shows are begging me for my audience. Mind you, at the time of building my audience, this wasn't my intention. As I've stated before, YouTube was an outlet for my creativity; it gave me happiness, and it was a hobby. It still does. If no one watched me again, I'd still make YouTube videos because they help me release emotion and help me express my feelings the best way I know how.

I like to post healthy body image videos because I find that it's the one thing I get thanked for the most on my posts these days. "Thank you, Trish, for helping me love my body." "Thank you, Trish, for showing me that I don't have to be a size 0 to be beautiful." "Your confidence inspires me." How this started? I don't really know. I didn't start posting pictures to show my confidence. Heck, I didn't even realize that's what that was. Because I'm not a size 2 and I'm showing my stomach, I'm confident? Maybe, but I just consider it living my life in the body I have, you know? You don't find confidence; confidence finds you. You start taking pictures of yourself and checking yourself out in the mirror, and that confidence just comes around because over time haters will get bored with you; you'll get bored with haters, and you're both still going to be living your lives.

Set a good example for others by taking pride in your appearance and not apologizing for it. If people say that you wear too much makeup, chances are they wish they knew how to enhance their face the way you do. If someone tells you that you need to eat a sandwich, chances are that he or she struggles with being uncomfortable in his or her body. Whenever someone else feels the need to judge you or tell you how you need to be, there's something internal going on with that person.

When I show a video of my house, people will notice all the pictures of myself on my wall in my living room and kitchen. My bedroom is full of pillows with my face on them, and my office is decorated in fan art sent to me by you all. I like to look at myself; I think I'm the most beautiful piece of art, so why not gorge myself in beautiful art? My body reminds me of those goddesses I used to love to read about in mythology class. Aphrodite is the goddess of love, beauty, and sexual rapture, so as far as I'm concerned, that's beauty in the oldest form. What does your body remind you of? When I was about thirty pounds heavier, my body reminded me of fluff, and I loved it. I know that sounds crazy to some people, but fluff is the one food that made me happiest growing up. I loved the way it looked, tasted, expanded. I also had a pillow that looked like fluff that was the most comfortable pillow. I slept on it for fifteen years and it never did get old (an ex-boyfriend actually stole it). I still danced on occasion at the strip club when I had the "fluff" body. I wasn't able to dance in Hollywood with it, but I found a club in the valley that took me, and I was the top earner. I know that the validation of getting the most dances wasn't the cause of my confidence; it was more due to the fact that I just loved my fluff. What some may call fat, I saw as fluff, and I loved it. My body just matured into Aphrodite. The older I get, my body seems to sort of tone itself out. I have to walk more just to get energy in the morning, and it's really shaped me out. The baby fat in my arms and cheeks is what I've noticed to be leaving first. There's nothing I can do to stop my body from maturing how it wants, but there's nothing I'd want to do to stop it from evolving. I rock my Aphrodite body, and if you want to say that it's a whale, well then you're going to have to answer to Zeus about that. Good luck!

Molest yourself. I love touching my body! Not even in a sexual way, but I love to pet my legs when I'm lying on the couch and feeling my skin. We all have different skin textures, and by knowing your skin and how it feels, you'll start wanting to embrace that skin more. Even if you're wearing a turtleneck and long underwear, there's a confidence that can radiate when you know how wonderful your skin is. Once you are truly comfortable in your skin, others will acknowledge that and have nothing to say. There was a time when I would sit down, and every time, just by habit, I would cross my arms over my stomach in an effort to not show rolls. Newsflash, teenage Trish, everyone has rolls when they sit down—well at least 99.3 percent of the population does. By crossing my arms in front of me, it made me look even more uncomfortable, looking back, which gave reign for the vultures to attack. The narcissist in me now wears shirts two sizes too small because I want everyone to see exactly what I'm working with, and that I don't give two shits if you don't find it attractive. I like to stick out my bust and flaunt my tits and wear so much makeup you can't even see my eyes because that's how I like it. It's not normal, and I do get strange looks and whispers, but keep on talking because while they are wasting precious moments of this precious life hating on me, I'm strutting on and not giving a single one of my incredible thoughts to them. It's like, "You're welcome for making your life interesting for these five minutes that I'm gracing your world with my presence." Swerve.

So have you taken a selfie yet since reading this? Will you? Will you take one for me, showing me what you're most proud of? I like freckles. When my sister is wearing no makeup, she has freckles all over her little nose, and it makes her so beautiful in my eyes. She's more confident covering them with makeup, and that's totally great, but if I had freckles, I would let everyone see them. Freckles on the face remind me of little sparkles of glitter. I used to wear glitter on my face, not even my eyelids, because they reminded me of freckles. I just think it's such a unique feature that not everyone has. I also like different colored eyeballs, soft bellies, and babes in bikinis. FYI, I think that every girl on planet earth is a babe—true story. I will see a girl in a bikini and just stare at her body, no matter if she's skinny, fat, or somewhere in between. I find the comparison to things I like as we talked about earlier. I love Kate Moss, and when I do see a really thin girl, I'm reminded of her body type, and I think it's so beautiful. Obviously, I'm partial to blondes with big tits because of my fondness for dolls when I was a little girl. When I see tall chicks, I'm immediately envious that they can be runway models and eat more and still look elongated, plus there's something so elegant about tall women. Uma Thurman, to me, is the epitome of beauty. She's extremely tall and just so graceful and looks like such a woman of power and dominance. I also had a fondness for the more unique beauties, like Juliette Lewis and Winona Ryder— the ones who have this beauty that radiates in anything and everything they do. There's something unique about those ladies, just like there's something unique in all of us. So maybe you don't have a perfect imperfection, but you might have that "it" that no one else knows about or knows exists. It's that "it" in you that makes you beautiful. It's that "it" in you that you need to flaunt, and that you need to brag about. You need to show the world that they're missing out on your kind of beauty if it's not already out there. And if it is already out there, well, you're already ahead of this narcissistic game, and we can just get right on to the next chapter!

CHAPTER 5

Love the World;
Spread the Love

❧

Now that you are head over heels in love with yourself and know how superior you are in this world right this moment, it's time to spread the love. It's true what they say: it is better to give than to receive, and one of the greatest lessons I've learned in life is that the more you give, the more you really do receive.

When I find myself getting negative, I stop myself right in my self-loathing tracks. The minute I start to feel sorry for myself is the minute I go out and do something for someone else. Fortunately, with my YouTube channel, I'm able to go and help quite a few girls with one video, but even if you can just help one, that's a good start. If I'm feeling depressed, I find myself writing a list of things that either make me happy already or that will make me happy if I start. I have a list of hobbies that I want to begin, but when I'm happy in my life, sometimes I just sort of leave those to the side. Does that make sense? For instance, YouTube is a hobby that makes me happy all the time. I love it, so I do it; that's one of those on my list of "already making me happy" hobbies that I'll always go to when I'm sad. However, something like knitting I'll put aside because it's out of my comfort zone, and if I'm already comfortable, why start doing it? Well the greatest thing about having hobbies that you never followed through on is that when you do hit those lows in life, you'll have something to fall back on to pick you up. My hobby to-do list is a mile long, and I love it. That means that for the next one hundred low points, I'll have a new adventure to start. This is exactly how I picked up current and past hobbies, such as YouTube and banjo and tae kwon do and movies and makeup. Some hobbies you'll continue; others, you won't. But either way, it's occupying your mind, leaving no room for negativity and depression.

Along those lines, when you are helping others, you end up helping yourself. When I do "self-help-type" videos on my channel (such as, "Your Body is Beautiful" or "Beauty at Any Size"), I start off doing them because I'm not feeling beautiful. I film them to remind myself how beautiful I am. For some reason, watching myself on film makes me realize how gorgeous I am. Narcissistic bitch, right? It really is the truth, though. I've taken all these steps to get to the point of loving myself, and sometimes I forget in moments of weaknesses. When you're feeling sad, you don't feel like looking in a mirror, but you should. When you really look at yourself and reflect on all that self-love we learned earlier, you're instantly back into that mode of "I'm worthy of everything in this world."

I digress. I filmed those videos at the start from a place of negativity, but by the end, I found this huge leap of happiness. The fulfillment comes from the fact that after I shared, after I posted them to my channel, I would receive instant feedback from girls saying how much this video was needed for them. In my heart, I feel like they felt my own transformation when I filmed those, and they could relate. Now, not only was I feeling happier for filming and watching my beautiful self back, but I was happy that I was making other people in this world happy. That's the most important thing to me. As an adult, I say that I struggle with self-hate—maybe once every few years, usually when I'm ready for a change, and it only lasts a few days, sometimes even only hours. The same cannot be said for when I was a teen, and that is why I feel happiest when I'm helping teen girls transition their minds into a life of happiness and self-worth. Does that make sense?

Let's take a look at another scenario of giving back to the world. Maybe you don't have the voice to inspire others, or maybe people are just not your thing in general. That's okay; you can spread the love in other ways. It can be as simple as not spreading hate. Honestly, we live in a day and age where it's a surprise if someone is not mean to you. Whenever I get a compliment, I'm taken aback at times. I have to remember to say, "Thank you" and not, "Why are you saying this?" "What do you want?" or worse, deny the compliment. "Your hair looks really nice today." "Oh no, it's a mess; I didn't have time to wash it." That's another huge problem right there. Take the compliment; accept the love because this world needs more love, for sure, no doubt. So if you're thinking of a way to spread the love but can't figure it out, start with not spreading hate. Never speak words of hate on yourself or anyone else; that's the downward spiral that will escalate quickly. To quote the great Cher, "Words are like weapons; they wound sometimes." You can't take back words, and words will stick with a person for a lifetime. All of my complexes that I had to overcome stemmed from hurtful words. Even to this day, I'll remember those words. So please be careful with what you speak.

One of my favorite ways to spread the love in this world is through hugs. I believe hugs cure all. There have been times when I was crying or sobbing, and all I needed was a hug. A hug symbolizes to that person that he or she is not alone, that there is someone who will embrace him or her in this world. Even if you're not close to a person, if they're opening up to you, hug them. I remember that a girl at the strip club I worked out found out that she was three months pregnant. She wasn't crying, but she was acting really tough about it. I was doing my makeup, and she was on the phone. She told whoever was on the phone that she was going to give it up for adoption. When she got off the phone, I didn't make eye contact with her, but she was really short with me for no reason. She asked me something along the lines of why I was listening to her personal conversation. I kept quiet. The manager came in and told her that she had to go on stage, and she was really combative with him about not wanting to perform right then and being really nasty. He told her that she'd be fired because we were short some girls. That's when I volunteered. She continued to be nasty and said that she didn't need my pity. I said, "It's not pity. I need the tips." The manager left, and she went quiet and just looked at me as though I were a ghost. I smiled; she smiled, and that's when I gave her a hug, and she started crying. I had never talked to that girl prior, but I knew that she needed someone to just let her know that this world is okay; she was okay; everything is okay.

The best part about spreading the love when it's genuine is all the love you get back. I do get a lot of hate online, but the love outweighs the hate by the gallon. I don't make videos to harm people. Some of them may be satire videos that people don't understand, but that comes from humor, which is, of course, subjective. I love social media because you can tweet out words to strangers that could change their lives.

In general, if you're a positive and loving person, people will want to be around you. Nobody wants to be around a complainer. Instead of saying, "Why me?" in tough situations, ask yourself, "How am I going to overcome this?" Experiencing heartache, pain, suffering, will only make you stronger. As Josephine Hart said, "Damaged people are dangerous; they know they can survive." I think that's how I got to be so fearless in life. In my personal journey, I should've been dead on at least three different occasions. I've gone down dark paths and have come out in the light. I see the light; I've been to the light, and now that light is in me. I know no words can break me; no person can take me; and God will save me. Light attracts light. The light radiates through. When you do good unto others, it makes you more attractive in every sense of the word. You'll have this inner light that will make your physical beauty shine and your inner beauty visible. It's a crazy thing, positivity. Positivity will attract what you need and give others what they want. Positivity is a choice. Happiness is a choice. Maybe your circumstances in life aren't ideal right now, but that doesn't have control over your personal well-being. Remember to pay it forward. You're struggling right now; try to help someone else and push forward in life. Focusing on others will take focus off your own problems and will allow good fortune to find its way into your life. If you're consumed with troubles, there's no room for rewards to come in. Free your mind of bad, focus on good, and it's really that simple.

This world is a beautiful place. The news will often emphasize the bad because that is what sells. Only around the holiday season do we see the Good Samaritan stories, and that's an unfortunate thing. I've met thousands and thousands of people in my lifetime from all over the world; I know there is more good than evil. This life is worth living because you're in it. You're not here by mistake. You're here for a reason. This world is better because of you, and you can better this world. There are days when I feel low or sad, but I still thank God for allowing me to wake up, for putting air in my lungs. There is a reason why He does this. I love life so much, sometimes I cry. It's not because my life is perfect all the time—so far from it—but there are so many opportunities to be had, people to touch, food to taste, adventures to go on, things to try, memories to share—this life is too good. We are lucky that we are given such a gift, that we made it onto this earth. Do you know how many are not as lucky? Never take this life for granted and always show your thanks to this world, to this earth, to others, and to yourself. Smile and open up your heart. Times get tough, but it's how you handle them that makes you this ultimate human being. If you can get through the tough times, the most amazing times will be that much more wonderful for you. I know that I am appreciative to be alive. As I mentioned before, life is still the only gift I could ask for. I've known death, seen death, and been on death's door. How I made it out, I'll never really know or understand in this life, but I am so happy I did. I am so *very* happy I did. I think that going through that made me see life in a whole different way, and I try to share my vision on life with others who may have not gone through the same experience, nor would I wish that on anyone. I think that sometimes a few of us have to go through those hardships to share with others so that they do not. God gives us all different challenges for a reason; sometimes we may never understand. Never lose faith though. That's the biggest lesson. God has given me so much unconditional love, and I want to fill you all with the same amount of it.

Love this world. Spread the love. Show the world why you're here and show yourself why you're worthy of the extraordinary life that you are destined for. Live this life to the fullest. It's okay to have regrets, just don't dwell on them; learn from them. If we have no regrets, how do we grow and become stronger?

You are given one life. Don't waste it. Embrace it. Love it. Live it.

CHAPTER 6

Superficial Bitch

Okay, are we feeling spiritual? Are we all for one love, baby? Peace, love, and dope. Just kidding. Sometimes when I go beyond myself and start talking about my love for God, it can come off as a little hippie-dippie, but I love it, so who cares, right?

Now don't get it twisted, I believe that helping others is the single most important thing we can do on this earth as human beings. But just because you help others, don't forget to help yourself.

My biggest milestone to self-love was being a superficial bitch. I know this sounds bad, but it's not. I don't buy things because commercials tell me to, celebrities endorse it, or society says I need it—no fucking way, man. I buy things that make me happy. I do like to shop; I'm a shopper for sure. It's a hobby I picked up during a really sad time. I do love it, and it gives me these unexplained endorphins. However, even if you don't shop as a hobby, shopping for yourself will be the physical representation of showing yourself how much you are actually worth.

I've been talking a lot about self-worth throughout, and that's what we're all trying to understand. I know I'm worth over a billion dollars; in fact, there is not enough money in all the world to be able to buy who I am, what I stand for, and what I look like—it's just never going to happen. So if I'm worth more than all the money in the world, why can't I spend a grand on myself once a year for new clothes? Why can't I spend a few hundred dollars a month getting my nails and hair done? That's pennies compared to my actual worth. By spending money on yourself, you're doing a physical manifestation that you're worthy of hard work. You earn money by working hard, and well, you should reward yourself with some of it. Don't forget that responsibility and bills are a priority, but just budget what you can to make sure that you are right on top with those to be a priority as well.

Literally, I have a monthly budget that includes bills (rent, phone, food, gas, Internet, cable, electricity). These are my necessities. Yes, Internet and TV are necessities—don't judge. Also on that priority of things I must budget is entertainment and beauty. I have to go out to the movies once a month and have to get my hair, nails, and waxing done once a month. Also a priority is a one hundred dollar allowance on frivolous buys. This has been my monthly budget since I have lived on my own as of the age of eighteen. I make ten times the amount now that I was making when I was eighteen. When I was eighteen, before

I started stripping, I made $1,500 a month, and I was still able to budget my frivolous buys and beauty regime because it was important to me. I had to make sacrifices elsewhere. I was living in a studio apartment with no windows, but I made it cute and girly, and that was fine by me. I knew that if I didn't feel good about my outer appearance like I didn't when I was younger, I would never find a better paying job, the significant other I wanted, etc. It doesn't get more superficial than this, but my blonde hair gives me superpowers. I'm not kidding. Ever since I started bleaching my hair blond, no matter what shade of blond it is, I feel like I can conquer the world. I like the way it looks physically on me, but I like the way it makes me feel. It feels like Trish. For some reason I've always been attracted to blond hair; it's just something that is. It's not for everyone, but for me it represents myself to a T. Blond hair is fun and bright, and Barbie had it, and Barbie did everything in life. She had every career, and well, so have I. It's just me. Even though I always get that I should dye it dark, stick to my natural color, let it be healthy, stop damaging it, you'll look more attractive, blah, blah, blah, I just would not because it doesn't make me happy. One time, I went red, and I cried for days. I didn't want to leave my house or see anyone, and I didn't. I didn't leave my apartment for thirty-one days–true story. I had to wait till I could afford to fix it, but I was devastated. I know that sounds so superficial, and it is, but we have to see ourselves every single minute of every single day, so we'd better be happy with our appearance.

The most important step for a beginner superficial bitch is to find that one outfit that makes her feel like a goddess. The dress I wore on *America's Got Talent* was my goddess dress. I got a lot of hate when I wore it on national TV. Some said that it was too tight, not flattering, looked cheap, but I loved it, and I loved the way I felt in it. After that appearance, a lot of people asked how I was able to go up on that stage and do what I did, and I'm telling you that it was that dress. I strutted onto that stage because I wanted the whole world just to see me in that dress. I had that dress for a good four years prior. I actually wore it in the "All American Rejects" music video for *The Beekeeper's Daughter* as well. I wore the heck out of that dress and retired it right after *America's Got Talent* because there was no way that dress could top that moment. I still have it in my closet. When I went back to be on the finale of AGT, they specifically asked me to wear that dress. I rest my case.

Get an amazing dress to wear everywhere. Forget the rule that you can't be photographed in the same thing twice. For goodness sake, I wore it for two major Hollywood jobs and then some. Who cares? Wear it and rock it. That pink dress was only like fifty dollars, if that. So it doesn't have to be expensive to make you feel like a rock star.

Superficial bitch, stage two: the accessory. Okay, so now I have like five accessories that Trish must have at all times, but when I was younger and not making a lot of money, the one accessory I had to splurge on was MAC lip gloss. MAC gloss made me feel like I was rich. For some reason, I liked the feeling of being rich when I was younger, even though I wasn't. I guess that in the inside I felt so superior to people that I wanted to show them my self-worth on the outside. When I wore an eighteen-dollar lip gloss on my lips, I felt like I could conquer the world. Even though other people probably had no idea that I was wearing MAC "Myth" gloss, I knew it, and that's what gave me that extra pop in my step. So if you can't afford to splurge on multiple items, splurge on one thing that will make you happy every time you use it. It really does wonders. I bought my first designer bag last year when I was twenty-four. It was a Louis Vuitton Speedy, and I never felt more on top of the world. I worked hard for it, and I loved it. Whenever I wore it out, I felt like it represented my hard work, my struggle, my achievements, my worth. It showed the world what I was capable of, but most importantly it showed me what I was capable of. When I was younger, I would trash on Louis Vuitton because never in my life did I think I'd be able to afford it. I would say that it's ugly or that it's easily knocked off because I didn't see it as a possibility for me to own. The bitterness I felt was a poor reflection of myself for thinking that I could never work hard enough to own one. So when I bought it, I did shed a little tear, not going to lie. I always thought I'd be one of those girls who'd marry a well-off man and have babies and be taken care of; I thought that was the only way I would ever prosper in life. I don't knock that lifestyle, and I think it's wonderful for those who live it or who stumbled upon it, but I feel very proud that I was able to make something of myself by myself.

To be a superficial bitch is something you should do for yourself and never for others. If you try to change to please others, you're going to give all that power of happiness and self-love to them, and you'll lose control. Please don't do that.

We just spent six chapters giving the control to you, so when becoming a superficial bitch, keep in control. I'm at the point where I don't even ask others' opinions on clothes or bags I buy because, who knows, they could be that same "bitter Betty" I was when I couldn't afford a certain item.

So the next time you see a girl with a certain swag, know that she's a superficial bitch. The next time you wonder how I'm always happy, remember that I'm a superficial bitch. Whenever you need a confidence boost, become a superficial bitch. Yeah, I said it: the world depends on us superficial bitches taking over. Now go be superficial, bitch.

CHAPTER 7

We All Have Those Ugly Days

✺

O kay, babe, listen, we all have those ugly days where we are going to just feel fat or ugly no matter what we look like or what anyone tries to tell us. These ugly days are inevitable and happen to even the most seemingly perfect person. Sometimes ugly days turn into ugly weeks, and over time, you may just think that you're ugly because of stupid comments from people who don't have to live your life. Think of it like this: if people are commenting on your latest social media pic or what you're wearing in real life, they must not have a life. Why would it matter to them what you wear, if your arms are toned, or if you're eating healthy or not? The thing is, it doesn't, but they are projecting their own insecurities. You really must never forget this. They may be going for an easy target. Yes, it's easy to pick on my weight because I'm not a size 0. It's clear; I am a thicker girl, so it is the easiest and lowest "blow." And I say "blow" in quotations as if I give two shits. What some may see as "flaws" in me I see as what makes me special.

I'm a curvy girl. A lot of people like to say that I'm fat, so I say I'm fat. By taking away that power of that word, they have no more ammo. If I say, "I'm fat and fabulous," that comment, "Oh yeah, but you're still fat," can't exist anymore. It's pure science, baby.

Accept your flaws. If you can't see your imperfections as fabulous, at least accept them. To accept your flaws is to accept yourself. So when people try to bring you down with your flaws, you'll no longer care because you've already accepted them. How do you accept something that society, family, and friends may see as a hindrance in your life? Evaluate who is telling you this, what they are telling you, and why.

Who is saying this to you? Is it your family telling you that something about you isn't good enough? If it's your family, you may think that they are telling you something because they care about you, which may be true. But from experience, I'll tell you that my family has never once told me to lose weight or to change my appearance. Why? Because they accept me for who I am. I am an adult with knowledge on what's appropriate, what is healthy, etc. If your family doesn't fully accept you for who you are, that is their problem. They are probably unhappy that they can't live the way you do. People who critique others often wish they had the ability to live without inhibitions. Family will usually come around, and often they don't say criticism out of a place of hate but out of a place of not knowing. Your ability to love yourself even though you're not perfect will scare a lot of people. This unknown confidence is something that people will fear and envy and therefore try to get you to change, to be more insecure about your insecurities. Does that make sense? Now, let's say that the person telling you what you need to change and why comes from the Internet, an anonymous post, or someone you've never even met before. First of all, why do you even care what someone who doesn't know you thinks of you? Second, the Internet is a place where all negativity will go unpunished. It literally gives people free reign to say whatever they want to whomever they want. They'll point out your flaws all day long because they need attention. They are envious that you can post a picture of yourself, and they can't because they are scared. Or they need attention in the form of socializing. A lot of these Internet trolls probably live at home with their parents; they may be teenagers with no friends or middle-aged men who never could make it on their own. Whichever it is, they are craving interaction, and unfortunately, on the Internet, negativity will garner the communication they so desire. So do not feed these trolls. Hit that block button or, better yet, let them ride and obsess over you. If someone hates you based on what you portray yourself as on the Internet, he or she obviously wants something you have. Especially if that person keeps coming back to hate. If you truly hate someone or someone truly disgusts you, you eliminate that from your life; you don't consume yourself with them. You only consume yourself with somebody that deep down you want to be associated with or compared to or idolize. Think about that.

Now listen to what these people are telling you. Are they telling you that you need to change your appearance? Are they telling you that you need to hide something you're flaunting? By looking at what people are telling you, you'll have a better understanding to help them with their own insecurities, which we have already established as the reason that they are concerning themselves with you in the first place. If people are telling me to lose weight because I look like a pig, I go see what they look like. Nine times out of ten they are extremely overweight, and I can see the hurt that they feel because of it. They, for some reason, can't allow themselves to embrace who they are, extra weight or not. It makes me sad for them. Instead of patronizing them or talking down to them or offering my direct help, I figure that the best thing I can do for them is to keep taking pictures of myself and doing so in ways that are not always flattering. By continuing to take pictures of my body—my "overweight" body, if you will—I'm showing them that the worst that can happen is that people will say mean things to you, and it won't affect you. I think people are often scared to embrace their flaws because they are worried about what people might say. Yeah, people might be mean, and yeah, people may snicker, but if you don't care, pretty soon they won't either. I continue to post pictures to hopefully show them that they, too, can do the same, and their worst fear of someone saying something mean about their body (like they say to me) is really not all that scary.

Then you have to look at the why they are saying what they are saying. If they are posting hate on a social media post, they are being hateful for two reasons: boredom and attention. You have to just look past this. If your friends are passing judgment on your appearance, personal preferences, personality, etc., the why is extremely important in this case. Why would a friend tell you to lose weight, or why would a friend tell you that what you're wearing is ugly? Because they are not a true friend. The sad truth in life is that we associate with people who don't have our best interest at heart all the time. It's why I am very selective who I let into my life and who I call a friend. The minute a "friend" tells me that I'd look better skinny or that I shouldn't wear a certain thing, I slowly distance myself. I do not need that negativity in my life, and neither do you.

We all have our own demons we must face. To have someone else project their demons on top of ours is very unhealthy. You're going to struggle with your looks and choices throughout life; as I mentioned earlier, this is inevitable. We all are going to want to better ourselves because we're never going to be the perfect human being. But that is okay because we only have to be the perfect us. I wanted to conclude this chapter with one of my favorite blog posts I published earlier this year:

> *I always wanted to be Malibu Barbie, but God didn't quite create me that way, so I turned into my own kind of Barbie, my favorite kind: a li'l Trish Doll-me.*

So I was going through my candids of a photo shoot I had last week for the cover of my next book, and I was looking at all the untouched random iPhone photos and wanted to post some, but I thought, "hmm, my arm looks huge, and my legs look pudgy; my butt is too wide and not enough of a bubble; people are gonna say I have cankles; my bra is showing; wish I knew how to photoshop my personal pics, etc. "

Then I relooked at 'em this morning, and I saw so much beauty in these pictures. I saw a girl who was having fun living out her dream of not only accomplishing a finished third novel but getting to be the cover model for it in her backyard in a Southern California beach city, which is literally the sand at my doorstep. I saw this girl who, yeah, had a little bit of fat on her, but that fat meant that she could now afford to eat on her own, when in the past she had to either starve or rely on men to get her food. I looked at this picture and saw legs that weren't skinny but strong. These legs walked me out, nay, they ran me out of some dangerous situations. And mostly I saw a smile that showed how happy I truly am in life right now, regardless of what people think of my size, my fashion, my hair, my life, my choices.... I had a legitimate genuine smile, and some of these poses, I don't think a lot of girls would be able to do because they don't believe they are sexy. This is the pose of a girl who *knows* she is sexy and it's taken me twenty-five years to be fully aware of my *sexy* and fully able to flaunt it with no apologies and no photoshop!

I just wanted to share this because I know a lot of us curvy girls struggle with "Should we lose weight? Should we not?" At the end of the day, it's your decision, and it's whatever makes you happy. Do you wanna feel better? Do you wanna look better? Do you think losing weight will help with that? *Then do it.* But don't forget to look at yourself right now and appreciate all that has gone into that body you have today: the stress you had to endure, the heartache you've experienced, the happiness you've celebrated. The body you're in today has quite the story. So while you may want to create a new beginning or not, never forget or be ashamed of the story which you've already written.

CHAPTER 8

Do It in Public

One of the best things I ever did for my self-confidence was to become an exhibitionist. I know this sounds crazy, and I don't recommend that everyone go take their clothes off, but when I was able to take my clothes off in a strip club and be completely naked in front of men and women and not only be naked but flaunt my naked body, it was completely liberating. When I started to get into modeling, I was asked to do a lot of niche modeling–plus-size lingerie. A lot of this lingerie was something that I would never have thought I'd wear much less be the one to sell it to the masses by wearing it on my body. I often wondered why these companies kept picking me over the "real" plus-size models. (The standard is five feet ten, 160 pounds.) I was short and a little tacky with my platinum blond hair. I asked the photographer of my first major shoot for a lingerie company that sold in all major sex stores why they picked me. He told me that it was confidence. He told me that I was the only one who came into the go-see and wore anything and didn't ask questions or try to modify it. The first go-see I went on for that particular company was in their warehouse in downtown LA. They wanted me to try a different option with a certain pair of panties, and I just threw off the top right there and waited for the next one with my, at the time, uneven, saggy breasts completely exposed. I know a lot of models who request to go into a bathroom to change, but on a set, you don't have that time to waste. Everyone is a professional on these sets; everyone has seen what you've got—ten times over. Plus-size models in particular, I've noticed, have this issue. When I went into the audition for the Eminem video, I wore the bikini that we were requested to wear underneath my clothes. A lot of girls told casting that they forgot one or that they would send pictures. This showed their lack of confidence, and nobody wants to work with that. That lack of confidence will always translate through. That's why if you go into your local sex store and see my boxes of lingerie, you'll notice that I have big happy smiles on all my shots because I felt good in the lingerie, and I was proud to be wearing it, showing other girls of my size that it's okay to be proud of being a queen size. It goes back to what we were talking about in the last chapter of leading by example. I'm this size, and I'm flaunting it, and you can too.

Now you don't have to be a stripper or model to get over your insecurities. I'm going to focus on the insecurities of being a curvy girl. Every summer when "bikini season" rolls around, a lot of us bigger gals feel like we can't wear a two-piece for whatever reason. Here's the thing: they make bikinis for larger women; thus, larger women are meant to rock the bikini. Again, if you put yourself out there completely exposed for the world to judge, the worst thing that can happen is that people make fun of you. Big whoop! They are not able to do what you're doing and ultimately not able to enjoy their life. What is summer if you can't wear a bikini? Are you going to sweat through T-shirts just because you're afraid of your arms jiggling? Cellulite? We've all got it—even the skinny bitches. If someone has a problem with it, they don't have to look. If someone has a problem with it and they continue to look, they are obsessed with you, babe; take it as a compliment.

When I see people stare at me, I never think it's because of my outrageous clothes or size or hair or what have you. I feel like they are staring at me because they are trying to figure out how? How can I be so confident? How can they be like me? How can I not give a care in the world that they are staring at me? Because I don't. I go out with people who aren't use to the stares, and they'll say to me, "Do you ever notice that people stare at you?" To be honest, I don't anymore. When I go out in public, I dress for me and me alone. If I feel good in it, I just focus on me that day. I do not have time or energy to worry about others. I don't even see others. I live in my own little Trish bubble, where I am a perfect Trish. I am the perfect specimen in Trish world, and if I were to gain one hundred pounds or tone up or go bald or whatever, I would still be perfect Trish. When you understand that, you are the perfect you; little things in life won't really worry you. Whether people stare or not is not my concern, but if I do see it or someone points it out to me, I amp up my strut ten times louder and do not hold it back. If they are going to look, I might as well give them something to look at, right?

Here's my challenge to you. Go out in public in something that you may not feel comfortable in. Go out in a bikini to the beach or bare your arms, legs, or tummy somewhere where there are a lot of people. If people stare, smile and strut. If people don't stare, the insecurities were probably in your head to begin with. There are times when I go out in clothes that I feel amazing in but will sometimes wonder, "Oh is this too much? Is this too tight? Should I wear Spanx?" Either way, I usually wear it. More often than not, in those outfits in particular, no one even gives me a second glance, which can also be a very calming thing. The point of all this is that everything is in your head. If you feel like a superstar, you are a superstar. If you feel less than a superstar, it's going to reflect but only in your head. Some people care what you look like; some people don't. That's why you've always got to live to please yourself.

CHAPTER 9

Fuck Society

If someone tells you that you're not good enough, fuck them. Seriously, fuck them. Who the fuck has the right to tell you what you're good enough for? God made you, and God made you not just good enough but great enough for everything and more.

For my curvy girls, society is always telling us how hot it is to be skinny. Covers are photoshopped of perfect body models because they are not skinny enough. Fuck society. Shirts saying "eat less" make me physically sick. There is no ideal perfect beauty. There is not. The perfect woman who is attractive to every single man universally does not exist and will never exist. I believe that this whole skinny trend is made up by society to make us all miserable and to just "extinct ourselves," the human race, from the planet. I also give a big "fuck you" to society when they try to define what is curvy. Oh, just because you don't have a flat stomach like Kim

Kardashian, you're fat; she's curvy. Bullshit. Curvy is curves—whatever, wherever those curves may be, okay? People have given me a ton of shit recently saying, "Trish, let's be real: you're not curvy; you're fat." Does that make you feel better about yourself? Okay, fine, I'm fat. Now let's talk about the curves. Big bellies are curvy. You go into an art class, and you will see rolls on the backs and fronts of the models. Why? Because curves give dimension to the art piece. Curves are visually appealing to the eye and amazing to the touch. I have a gut—I do—and that is one of the biggest curves that is drawn of me when someone sketches me; hence, I am curvy. I swear, our society gets dumber and dumber.

For my skinny girls, you are lucky that you are accepted by society, but if you have longed to be curvy, guess what? You are too! Look at yourself in the mirror, okay? Not that I have experience being skinny, but I look at my sister, who is my height but a good ninety pounds less than I. I look at the small of her back, which curves in right before her tiny little bottom starts. That is a beautiful curve—one of the most sought-after curves with the photoshop craze lately. You just have to find your curves if you want to see them. A woman's breast, no matter how small, is a curve. Around our areola is this little bit of "fat" that shows that we are a woman. I met a woman who had a mastectomy and no longer had this "curve," and she said that she finds her womanly curves through her scars. Her scars are puffy and projected, and she said that she went through a lot of pain and suffering for those. That shows her to be the strongest kind of woman there is. She didn't want to get her scars lasered off because they were her one curve. She said, and I quote, "Finally I have something on my body that I'm proud of." Talk about embracing your imperfections.

Here's the thing: society is nobody. Society does not exist. We are society. You are society. So no longer am I, nor do I want you, to say, "Society says this." Fuck society to nonexistence. Society wants us to crash and burn as a human race. Nope, sorry, that's going to be you, society.

Who are we really giving power to—lowlifes with an Internet connection? Fancy executives at magazines who were paid to say that something is attractive by a certain company? The power is in you, baby. The power to say that this is beautiful is in you, and it starts with you. If you can convince one person, even if it's yourself, that who you are is more than okay, you are changing this world. That confidence is going to be contagious. Share that self-love and spread that self-love and help others find theirs. Maybe you don't have to preach it, but lead by example.

Next time you look at a magazine and think you wish that you could look like that, think about how that person might look at you and think the same thing. Next time you turn on the TV and see someone talk about diet, remember: that's what works for them, and it may not be what works for you. You have no one to please but yourself. You have no one to answer to but yourself. And if you think for one minute that society's ideal of beauty defines you, oh, baby, you are worth so much more. Your beauty is unique. Not one other person in the world will ever look like you or be you. Even identical twins have their own uniqueness. Our DNA is something that is rare and exclusive to us. You are that diamond in the rough, so shine on.

CHAPTER 10

Bottom Line

Bottom line: you are beautiful. Your beauty is something I'm envious of. My beauty is something you are envious of, and we can all celebrate this beauty by being true to ourselves. If I leave you with one thing, it's this. True happiness comes from self-love. Once you can truly and fully accept yourself with all your imperfections, flaws, and shortcomings and still just love you for you in this day, you will be happy every single day of your life. When they say that happiness is a choice, it is because it is your choice whether or not you are going to love yourself. Don't focus on the negative; only focus on the positive, and positivity will flourish in your life.

Pretty soon, people will start wanting to know your secrets. These are mine. So feel free to take from this book what works for you because, again, this journey is all about you. You have one life—live it. Don't let weight, people's criticisms, or judgments hold you back—ever. The time on this earth is precious and so are the humans that inhabit it. So be nice to yourself and be nice to others. Fully loving yourself will mean that you'll never have a hateful thought in your mind again—isn't that a freeing thought? I gave you the key to happiness, and I gave you tips to love yourself. Why? Because I want you to be truly happy. That's all I ever want for anybody. I want us all to be oh so happy. I've known pain, suffering, and misery because I chose to feel those. Now I only choose to be happy. Life's little setbacks will happen, but when you are confident in yourself, knowing not only that you are beautiful but strong as well, you will get through anything. You will help others get through their hardships, and that is what this life is all about. That will be your legacy.

Big girl, you are beautiful. Skinny girl, you are beautiful. Girl, you are beautiful. Don't ever forget that you are loved; you are stunning; and you are worthy of everything you want out of this life and more. I want you to hug yourself and love yourself. When you think nobody else in this world loves you, remember that you love you, and that will be more than enough to get you through anything you're currently going through.

This is a journey, ladies and gentlemen. So don't feel like this self-love has to happen overnight. What can happen right now though is this: you can choose to be happy. Just say right now, "I am going to be happy," and you will be. You look in that mirror and smile at yourself. Smile at a stranger. I truly believe that a smile can change the whole world. After all, I think the smile is the sexiest curve anyone can ever have. Smile lots, and you're on the road to being curvy and loving it.

But wait—there's more!

With what I do, I get a lot of young girls and guys asking me for my personal advice on how to gain confidence, feel better about themselves, etc. I figured that I would throw in a sort of advice column in this book and answer some of the most frequently asked questions I get from my viewers and online followers. These questions range on topics covering everything from self-love to body acceptance and more! And if you ever see me in the streets or find me online, don't ever be afraid to ask me any questions. I talk about personal issues with you because I've been to the lowest point when it comes to issues with myself. My hope is to be able to share how I personally overcame my issues so that maybe you can find a nugget that relates to you and that will help you in this journey of ultimate self-love. A lot of my answers will probably have the hot points of this book incorporated as I feel like the chapters written are the ultimate guide for how to love the person that is you. Enjoy!

Frequently Asked Questions

❧

Q: **"What do you think about people who self-harm/cut? Do you have any advice on how to stop?"**

A: A beautiful girl tweeted me a picture of her self-harm wounds healing. Her exact tweet was: "I am stopping for you, and they're starting to heal. You're such an inspiration to me, Trisha. Thank you."

I was literally in tears from reading her tweet and seeing her cuts. I'm not in tears because I helped her but more because she did that to herself, thinking that she wasn't good enough or deserving enough of love, life, or whatever issues she is/was dealing with.

I spent some time looking at her Twitter profile. This girl looks happy and is absolutely stunning, and it just broke my heart for her that she would want to do that to herself. The bright side is that she has *stopped* cutting, and that means so much to me. Her wounds are healing, but that means that so is she as a person. That brought even more tears to my eyes.

I'm not sure how specifically I helped her, but I'm so glad I could, and she inspired me to write this answer to maybe help others, even if that's just one other.

And I met another girl at my book signing in Toronto back in August who had a similar story. Again, I won't say names or go into specifics, but she was a former cutter who also took a little time to know that she was worthy of *amazing* things.

Know this: EVERY SINGLE ONE OF US ON EARTH IS HERE FOR A REASON. There are *no* accidents in God's world. There are no coincidences.

YOU WERE MEANT TO LIVE AN EXTRAORDINARY LIFE.

Look, I've never been suicidal, nor have I self-harmed, so I can't pretend to know what you're feeling. But I have been severely depressed in life. I've been on medications for depression; I've self-medicated with drugs in the past, so I know what low feels like. I was a prostitute for three years of my life; I ended up in the hospital twice from drugs; my body has been used and abused; I've never been one to have a lot of friends or genuine boyfriends–just people who want, want, want and take, take, take from me.

But you know what kept *me* going? It was knowing that I was put on this earth for a reason. I knew in my heart that I was meant to do something great with my life—that these dark times were just temporary. I couldn't see the light, but I had *faith* that it was there, and I'm telling you that once you catch a glimpse of that light, every struggle you've had will be worth it, and you'll understand *why*. You may not understand it right now, but you will, I promise.

We all have our crosses to bear in this world. Jesus carried the cross that he was crucified on, don't forget that.

And don't let anyone tell you that your problems are insignificant. Just because there are kids actually starving in Africa or dying of AIDS, doesn't make your problems any less tough or difficult. Cope with them in a healthy way. Talk to adults and seek counseling. Going to church helped me tremendously. Meditate, find an activity you enjoy doing—whatever it is, you will get through.

You have to put up with a little rain if you want to see the rainbow.

And remember: WHAT DOESN'T KILL YOU MAKES YOU STRONGER!

If you are currently self-harming, *please stop!* If you feel that nobody loves you or wants you, they do. Maybe somebody is out there waiting to give you unconditional love that you don't feel you currently have. Please have patience. Nothing is more selfish than taking your own life. Suicide is a permanent solution to a temporary problem. The people you leave behind will be devastated. It's not fair when so many people love you, even if you don't realize it. Know that I love you, and God loves you. I pray for every single one of you each night. I do. When I say my prayers, I pray that the people who read my blog, follow me on social media, and helped me achieve this happiness I'm living now will find the same happiness in their lives. And I *know* that God will provide that for you.

Happiness is easy to find if you realize what happiness is.

It's not about being the prettiest, the skinniest, the most popular, or the richest. No, happiness is a choice you make every day. Even in my current state of living my dreams, I've had problems and headaches—everything from lawsuits to stalking. But you know what? I don't let that get me down either. I wake up *every single morning* and say, "Trish, you're up another day. Thank the Lord for that by praying and doing something positive with it."

PLEASE STOP CUTTING. PLEASE. YOU ARE WORTHY OF EVERYTHING YOU WANT AND DESIRE IN THIS LIFE. EVERYTHING YOU HAVE, EVERYTHING YOU WILL HAVE—YOU DESERVE IT.

I LOVE YOU SO MUCH.

Q: "How do you always stay so happy?"

A: I'm not always happy. Nobody is. I have my low moments. Here's the thing, which I touched on earlier. Happiness is a choice. You can choose to let life's setbacks and let downs hold you down, or you can choose not to. It's really that simple. Acknowledge your emotions but choose your attitude. Happiness is an attitude. Your job may not pay the best; your friends may turn out crappy, but your attitude is what matters. In fact, I personally sum up people based on their attitude alone. A person can be struggling in life; a person can be down on their luck, but if their attitude is one that is happy, that person will never show any of that. Happiness feeds happiness. If you choose to be happy, eventually you will start to feel happy. You will manifest that real feeling of happiness, even if it's just your attitude to begin with. Those negative emotions will be overpowered by happiness, and in the end, you can be happy all the time if you live by this rule.

Having said that, we can't be happy all the time. We are humans. You will have periods of complete self-loathing, but you have to be in tune with yourself to catch it, myself included. This life is a journey; therefore, we are always in a process. We're never going to be fully completed. In my faith, eternal happiness can only be reached once we are home with God anyhow, so I accept that fact that the choice to be happy will not always come easy for me, but it has become easier with each day and each challenge I face.

So all in all, I'd say I'm happy 95 percent of the time, which is pretty darn good. I choose happy. I feel happy. I am happy. And keep saying that to yourself; you'll eventually believe it!

Q: **"What is the first step in starting to love yourself?"**

A: You took the first step by reading this book. So that right there is you telling yourself that you are worth this happiness you are seeking. You loved yourself enough to seek out a "self-help book." Do you see what that means? You went out, paid money, read this; that means you invested your time, money, and thoughts into loving yourself, into learning how to better yourself. That's the very first step. So congratulations, you already conquered it! Chances are, if you've made it this far, you are way beyond the first step.

Also go buy a pair of jeans or some other clothing; invest in something nice and indulge yourself. Don't buy it a size too small; buy it for the size you are today. To love yourself, you must value yourself, and the best way to do that is to celebrate your worth! So go get something for that body of yours that you're living in today. This is a physical symbol to say that you are good enough as you are in this very moment. Then progress with where you've got to go from there.

Q: "How do you get to the point where you feel 100 percent confident about yourself?"

A: Again, to be 100 percent of anything in this life is just not really possible. I am a confident gal, but as I talked about, I have my insecurities, as we all do. I believe we are always going to find faults in ourselves because God didn't make any of us to be perfect in the way that we think of perfection. We are the perfect children of God, but that means that we are flawed. So flaws will never let us be 100 percent confident. You can however, be 100 percent love. You can look at your perfect imperfections and choose to love them anyway. When you see an imperfection or hear a nasty comment about how you look or how you are, it'll put a little dagger into your confidence; you'll lose a few self-esteem points. However, if you can love yourself enough to look past this, you will be 100 percent love. Love and happiness, I'm convinced, are really all you need in this life. I feel that people can die of broken hearts and sadness, so that's why it is so important to have both love and happiness. And the great news is that both of those can come solely from you, believe it or not. We've already established that happiness is a choice. Now you know that my confidence is really just love. I love myself enough to not care what others think. I love myself enough to accept the flaws. I love myself enough to wake up every morning, to step out into the world, to put myself out there, and to do it all, being myself. Love and happiness can equal confidence for most! It does for me. And while my confidence can be shaken or tested, if you will, my love and happiness will always be there to step in for repairs.

Q: "How can I get people to know that I'm confident?"

A: Confidence isn't something you say or do. Confidence is the way you carry yourself. The way to "get" people to know you are a confident person is to say nothing at all. I promise you: before this book and really my career on the Internet in general, I never thought of myself as a girl with all this confidence. It kind of is something that people just started labeling me with. All these questions on how to be confident, how to stay confident, and all the comments about wishing they were as confident as I am was kind of a shock to me because it's not something I preached, nor is it something I ever really acknowledged or felt. Does that make sense? What people see is me posting pictures and not giving a fuck. They see a ton of hate comments and me continuing to do what I do. By not letting other people hold me back, hinder me, or make me cry, I guess showed that I was confident. So it all comes down to what you exude—what you show. I don't have to post a picture of me in a tight dress with the caption "I'm so confident" or "my confidence is showing"; it's unspoken. That's what makes it real and genuine. Now I like to have fun and post pictures where I know that people are going to attack because my gut is hanging out, my belly button is showing, and my legs are not toned and use hashtags like #Perfection

#WhyAmISoPerfect because it throws people off. They see it's not working; that it's backlashing. Their hate isn't bringing me down; it's empowering me. As we talked about, haters are your biggest fans. No one is going to spend time tearing others down if there's no reason behind it. They want something you have, don't ever forget that. Whether it's a look or just a vibe you put off, it bothers them that they can't achieve that yet. My hope is for all Internet haters to find happiness, love, and confidence in their own selves and lives that they will not have to resort to digging into other people's journeys. I really do. I like to poke fun at the haters and call them out, but I do it out of love because, in the end, they deserve happiness just like you and I. It takes a lot more time and energy to be negative, writing and saying nasty comments, than it does to just be happy, where you can fully live and let live.

Q: **"How do you deal with shopping in a size 2 world?"**

A: This is a question I find very interesting because even though in the back of my mind I realize that the fashion world revolves around the size 2, I honestly don't think about that when I shop because I've always been a bigger girl. So it's just life for me to have a harder time finding clothes that fit properly. I see shopping as one of the biggest reasons girls get down on their weight. I think if stores made clothes for all sizes and didn't label them as "plus size," it would make a world of difference. That label of plus size can really hurt a young girl because she can't go to the same racks as her friends. When I was growing up, I would become really sensitive to clothing stores and clothing in general. I often thought that my mom liked my sister better because she would buy her more clothes at the mall when, in fact, my sister could shop at any store and find clothes that fit her. I had to shop at department stores only. The trendy stores didn't really fit my thighs right, so I had to often shop in the women's section of the major stores. I would be lying to say that this didn't affect me, but it did. And it did make me want to lose weight because of it.

Fortunately for me, as I got older, and the Internet generation that followed after me, online shopping became relevant, so it was easier to find clothes for the curvy gal. I also got creative and made my own clothes that the skinny girls would be jealous of. I remember making the red plastic jumpsuit from the Britney Spears "Oops! I Did It Again" video for my sixth grade lip-synch contest. It brought out a lot of haters who made fun of my body in all vinyl, but I loved it so much that I remember that moment as the first time not caring what others thought because I knew how much they secretly envied it. How did I know this? My brother who was in high school was getting questions on where I got my outfit. Girls in my sister's grade in the elementary school were telling my sister how famous I was. I remember my sister wanting to play in it. My tiny sister wanted to wear my clothes; it was a cool feeling. So sometimes when life hands you lemons, you've got to make a red vinyl catsuit.

Look, shopping in stores that are catered to the "normal" weight of society will make you feel a little bad, point blank. Just avoid these stores and find ones that work for you, your style, and body type. Seriously, with the age of all things cyber world, there are endless stores online that will fit your body and your tastes. I've been loving pin-up girl/vintage sites for very flattering dresses to accentuate what I love most about myself, my bust. If you like the idea of making something but are not the craftiest with a sewing machine, they now have sites like Etsy and eBay, where people will make the design/pattern you like in your size. I've given pictures to some of my favorite tailors on these sites, and they were able to construct it, never having met me. People always ask me where I get my clothes, and to be honest, I do get a lot of them specially made because I like a certain fit or a I like a certain style, and if the fashion world won't cater to me, I'll cater to myself.

In life, you've got to make your own shit happen. Your destiny is bullshit. You create what you want. I promise you: I have no qualifications or special skills or secret tricks on how to get success. I got success by running into walls and then running through them. I think a lot of this stubbornness comes from not being able to find clothes that fit me. The same thing happened as an adult: no one wanted to hire me; I couldn't find a job that made me happy, so I made my own job, followed my own passions. Sometimes we want to be normal, but I think it's way more fun to be different.

After all, who really wants to walk around in the same name brand T-shirt and denim shorts with generic flip flops as everyone else? Why do you think girls always try to hide where they got that cute new maxi dress? Because deep down everyone wants to be unique; so be unique! People are going to notice you more when you are doing something different. There's a reason cloning isn't possible because how boring is that? It's not natural; it's not exciting. You are you, and nobody else in this world will ever, ever be you—ever. So take advantage of that, okay? Okay!

Q: "When you're feeling down, how do you pick yourself back up?"

A: Pizza cures everything. Just go ahead, pick up that phone, choose the delivery option, and eat that pizza, baby. Well, this definitely works if you're an emotional eater like me—instant pick-me-up. Pizza will always be there for me, and it has never let me down.

Now if you're not that low where you need to eat your feelings or if food just doesn't do it for you (BTW, we can't be friends—just kidding), you might like to do what I do: I like to journal or pray or meditate. With journaling, you're visualizing your low point so that you can recognize it easier and make a choice to do something about it—to change your attitude, if you will. Also, by writing it down what you're feeling, it's a healthy release. Too long I was one of those people who bottled my emotions and held in what I wanted to say. Sometimes it's not always best to speak what you feel but to write it so it's calm and collected and won't hurt anybody. Praying is my direct line to God. God knows everything, He is all-knowing, but when I pray, I can listen and know Him back. I can feel a change in my being that only God can do. To have your soul feel lighter, that's God working His blessings. When I pray, I always feel better. Even if you don't think God is listening, He is. Sometimes you just have to be patient to see His plan, but He reveals it in his time. When I look back on my twenty-five years of life, I see so clearly why things happened in the order they did; it's all a plan. Even now, I often feel like I found where I'm supposed to be, and I know I'm supposed to be here now because God has placed me here. However, I know there is even more that He has in store for me, but I am so patient because I know it will be so good, and that He is always in control. So I can fully enjoy where I am now. When I'm feeling low, I pray, and I'm reminded that this too shall pass, and that it's all part of a bigger plan. As far as meditation, this is just sitting alone in silence with no thoughts. You don't have to sit Indian style and go "hummmmmmmmmm." You can chill out on your bed, breathe in your car in a parking lot, or curl up on your couch. Close your eyes. A lot of times, people will think I'm trying to sleep or nap because I will meditate anyway if I need it. At an airport, on a train, in a fast-food drive through; it's all true. Sometimes when things seem overwhelming or too much, clear it all out. I will admit that sometimes mediation does turn into nap time, which can also help you get out of your feeling-down slump. When things pile up or I start to feel pressure to get everything done, I choose to do none of it and sleep. Usually when I wake up, I have a sense of clarity, peace, or at the very least energy to get through whatever I needed to do. It's not procrastination; it's knowing yourself well enough to know when you need a pick-me-up.

Know what your personal pick-me-up is in your times of troubles. The whole theme of loving yourself is being in tune with you. This may take time; this may take trial and error, but that's okay. The pick-me-up is an important part of coping with the tough times of life.

Q: "How did you deal with being compared to slimmer girls in high school?"

A: I would find girls who looked like me in the media. Granted, at the time, there weren't many. But my teachers would compare me to old-time movie stars like Jayne Mansfield and Ann Margret. At the time, I had no idea who they were talking about nor did anybody else in my grade, but I researched them. I started seeing them as beautiful rather than just the current stars. I started modeling myself after them and their mannerisms. Did people think I was a freak? Yeah, I'm sure of it. But that's what got me through. I think that's why I wanted to be an actress to begin with: I wanted to be exactly them rather than just being me with inspirations of their spirit. Identify with the people you see as beautiful that have similarities to you rather than comparing yourself to people who are the opposite of you. If I compared myself to girls in my school at the time, I don't know if I would've made it in this world. It will make you severely depressed trying to be like someone you can never be. The good news is that there is beauty out there that you can aspire to be. High school is a very small slice of the real world. In fact, high school is hardly the real world at all. It's a bubble in a little, tiny, baby section of this big, wide world. It will magnify small-minded thinking and opinions. You just may be too big for that town and either need to expand their horizons or get out and show them what they missed out on.

Remember that these slimmer girls may not be entirely happy with their shape either. When I was in school over a decade ago, skinny and slim were in, but now we are getting back into a time when curvy is where it's at. So a lot of these girls may be struggling with the fact that they don't have a huge bust or big hips or a bubble butt. They may wish they had your figure. So while you're busy comparing yourself to them and feeling miserable, they're probably doing the same. It's better to know and accept the fact that we all have different body types. This has been true since the beginning of time. I will never understand why we try so hard to fit one specific mold when it's an unnatural thing to conceive in the first place. Stop fucking comparing yourself to anyone. You're not in competition. Life is not a race. Success will come to those who want it, earn it, and deserve it. Success isn't limited to the first one hundred people to win at life; it's available to everyone and anyone who is not afraid to go after it.

Comparing yourself to others who are slimmer is a waste of time. If you want to be slimmer, be slimmer. If you like the way you look, then who fucking cares? Trust me, I would have loved to tell teenage Trish this same advice. It's so much easier said than done, and sometimes it's just something that needs to be learned over time. Your weight will never hold you back in life as long as you don't allow it to. So keep moving forward. You won't be able to do that when you're standing still to compare your love handles with her rib cage.

Q: "What's your diet like?"

A: I eat whatever I want! I know that sounds crazy and it may not be the healthiest, so it's probably not the best advice, but food is one of the greatest indulgences of my life. It's my vice, if you will. I eat for pleasure, and I know a lot of people will disagree with me by saying that food is for nourishment and medicine alone, but I treat food as a hobby. I'm a foodie. I'd rather go the gym for eight hours and get to eat cake. Here's the thing: I do walk an excessive amount because I do eat an excessive amount. It is not healthy to just eat pounds of bacon in a sitting, but you wouldn't feel good if you did this either. When I know I've over indulged one day, I will find something healthier to eat the next. Not all healthy food tastes bad; I'm not anti health food. I love going to the organic market and picking up raw foods, like nuts and fruits. In fact, if you have a sweet tooth like me, I'll share that I've been substituting buying candy for an after-meal treat and getting something like cantaloupe or water-melon. The texture and the sugars from both of these foods are extremely satisfying to me, but I've only just recently dis-covered this because I was in the mind frame that all healthy food tastes bad. I eat these fruits because I like them, and they taste good. I usually only overindulge when I'm socializ-ing and because I know when I'm going to socialize and know I'm going to overindulge, I do monitor my caloric intake the weeks before, or I just add extra workouts. It's also important to go to a doctor for annual checkups or when something is ailing you. If I went to my doctor tomorrow for a pain or ache and he or she said that I had to change my diet to correct it, I would. My father had kidney stones a few years back, and they told him that limiting dairy will help his overall health and well-being. He's in his late fifties now, and everyone tells him he looks forty. His energy is better, and he walks more miles than I do every day. If you feel bad eating shitty foods, don't eat them. Eat what makes you feel good. I don't feel glutton-ous or ashamed after eating a pizza; I feel happy. That's why I eat it. If it makes me feel fat or bloated the next day and I don't want to feel that way, I go for a walk.

Please note I am obviously not a dietary expert or nutrition-ist by any means. This is just my personal diet. It makes me happy; I'm healthy, and that's all that matters—the key word being *me*. Others may tell you that what you're eating is not good for you, but if you're reading this book, you know what is good for you and what isn't. It's not for others to judge or con-demn you. Food is a very personal thing for each individual. It's the subject I'm most sensitive about, so please be considerate when talking about other people's dietary choices.

This is my diet: I eat what I want. If it makes me happy, I eat it. If it's going to make me feel bad, I don't. When I want to lose weight, I research lifestyle changes. When I'm happy with my weight, I maintain. I don't focus on numbers on the scale but rather the way I look and feel in my clothes. If something feels too tight on me, I will buy a size bigger. If I don't want to buy a size bigger, I will change my eating habits. I'm an expert at maintaining size at this point; losing it is a different struggle. It's always going to be my challenge in life to control my fluc-tuation in weight. I accept this. Other people have other strug-gles they deal with. One thing I will say is that I never let my personal struggle with my weight affect my overall love and happiness in myself. I accept the fact that I struggle with my size at times, but I love myself enough to know when I want to change it or if I want to change it. Right now, I wouldn't change a thing. I'm a human, and more specifically, I'm a girl, so that will change probably by next month. Something that won't change? Trish Paytas and who I am as a person. I'd look sexy at five hundred pounds or fifty pounds because I'm just that awesome, and if you haven't figured it out by now, so are you.

Q: **"Being in the public eye, how do the hate comments not affect you?"**

A: Because I've heard it all before, babe. I really have. There is nothing that would surprise me or shock me anymore. When you've been called everything from a "shiny, greasy, sweaty pig" to a "lard, lazy fatass" to "a slut who looks like she's infested with herpes and AIDS" to "the trashiest, shit-faced, pimply, slobby, mess" to "dumb bitch with daddy issues" to.... You get the point? I read comments all the time like this, but the fact is that I was called much worse in my schools I attended. When you've heard it all and you're still alive and thriving, you realize how little words affect you after a while. Words are just words to me. Fat means nothing to me. If it makes a person feel better to call me fat, okay, that's fine. I'm going to just continue with my modeling career appearing in your local sex shops on the cover of lingerie boxes and magazines. If it makes a person feel better to call me trashy, that's fine. I'm going to cry myself to sleep in my silk sheets with my designer slippers. John Waters once said something along the lines of (I'm paraphrasing here): having good tastes means you can appreciate the irony of bad taste; if you have bad taste, then you don't get it. I'm different; it scares people, and when people encounter the unknown, they feel the need to try to destroy it. However, if you can rise above the destruction, you show others that they can do the same, and that's how this world evolves. This world doesn't evolve from all of us thinking and looking the same; it just doesn't work that way.

I strongly encourage you to look at words written about you or spoken about you as just words. Words have meanings by dictionary standards, but words don't run your life. Words don't make you successful. Words don't define how beautiful you are. Words are just words that can be spoken by any idiot—literally any idiot. If mean comments are being said about you on the Internet, well then, honey, stop right there, laugh, and write that right off. The Internet is notorious for people with low self-esteem finding courage behind the anonymity of the keyboard. If mean words are finding you in real life, then you really are a force to be reckoned with. People are feeling your amazing energy, and it's either scaring them or threatening them. Never stop owning that feeling and that energy. The minute you stop owning your energy or dulling your shine is the minute you start losing yourself and doubting yourself and ultimately hating yourself.

If it's too much to handle, stay away from social media. It can be cruel out there. Yes, I do choose to be in the public eye, and when you choose this, you will be crucified. I believe it's worth it—the greater good, if you will. I don't delete mean, hateful, downright nasty comments because it shows that I cannot and will not let those meaningless words dictate my life and my happiness. I'm proud of my life, myself, my family, and my accomplishments; so yes, I will show it off. If that bothers someone or offends someone, well, that's their issue.

Being a public figure comes with some setbacks, but the power to inspire others to be themselves through just simply leading by example is the greatest gift I could ever have been given. I don't like the term "role model," but if I'm your role model for one thing, I hope it's just me being myself. I just want to show that it's okay to be different. It's okay to be vulnerable. Most importantly, it's okay to love yourself to the extreme. Flaunt you and show you and love you and never be scared of it. Let yourself flow. Let yourself live. Life is too short to worry about haters. Live for the "likes," not that spam. Live for the selfies, not the selfish. Live for your well-being and not for the words.

Q: **"Sometimes it's just hard to love yourself."**

A: This is not really a question, but I hear this a lot! Sometimes you can get down on yourself, but it should never be hard to love yourself. Why? Because God created you. Even if you are not a believer, don't you think it's extraordinary how human life is created—how we come into this planet? You think creating a life and giving birth to a child is nothing short of a miracle? You are here. You made it into this world. It's not an accident; it's not a coincidence. This alone makes you a winner at life. You're in this life; you're breathing; you have life; you are a winner, and that alone deserves self-love. That should be the very basics of it. If you're going to get down on yourself because of weight, money, family issues, that's one thing, but never *not* love yourself because of it. This world and this life are yours for the taking; you've got to step up every day and rely on yourself. You only have you in this world. That's the way you have to think. If all your support system disappeared tomorrow, what would you be left with? You. And you would have to fight for you. So please don't ever think that it's hard to love yourself. You are a miracle. I call myself God's daughter, and because Jesus was God's son, that's a huge standard to live up to and an honor I so gladly take. If you don't believe, know that you are a superstar, a winner, a life breather, a life conqueror, a superior species. There's something extra special in everyone who breathes oxygen.

Now if you get down on yourself, let's talk about that. You love yourself, right? Right? Good. When it's hard to motivate yourself or keep yourself going, sometimes love isn't all you need. We talked about this already: seek help from other self-lovers to set your mind right. Whether that's your parents, friends, counselors, teachers, pastors, or God himself, seek outside sources to talk things out. While I always like to rely on myself for most things, there is a reason for other people in your life as well. Use them and take advantage of them. We are here to help each other, not hurt each other. I truly believe that humans are good, and we all want what is best for one another, deep down. We just get caught up in aesthetics far too often.

Please never stop loving yourself. It's not hard. You are living life. You are loving yourself. You are breathing, bathing, feeding your body. You are loving yourself. You get up to go to school or work to better your life and your family's lives. You are loving yourself. Self-love is so easy. It's not about doing anything or buying anything; it's about existing. Existence is so underrated. We exist for a reason—for a purpose. We were chosen. You were chosen. You've got to love yourself and give yourself a big ol' hug for that one. Did you hug yourself? Please do it right now. Please. It's super fun. I got super warm doing it, and then I squeezed tightly and then smiled because I realized how ridiculous I am. And I love myself for that. Don't you love yourself for taking time out of your life to squeeze yourself? If you can, go squeeze the heck out of someone else for no reason; they'll love it—unless they don't. At least you'll smile. Affection is so wonderful. I truly believe affection is a necessity of life: food, water, shelter, and affection. That's why little babies will die if they are not held. The same thing goes for adults: we become depressed without affection. So if you have no one to give you any (as is the case for me, sometimes), you give it to yourself—not sexually, you perverts. I mean, you can if that floats your boat. But just hug yourself. I cuddle myself at night with my arms around my tummy in the fetal position; it just feels so good. Is this getting sad? I hope not; it really makes me happy—especially after this full plate of spaghetti I made for dinner; I'm going to sleep well tonight.

Q: "How should you deal with people who criticize your weight?"

A: Hmm. Okay, great question. So write down all their critiques. Write down who said it and when and why. Now crumple that paper up and delete that person from your contacts and life because you don't need that shit.

What I will never, ever for the life of me understand is why your weight, my weight, or anyone's weight matters so much to another person. I don't buy that bullshit, "I'm worried for your health." Bitch, I don't want to die either; what the fuck, you know? I'm a grown-ass adult who has completed bullshit high school where we had to sit through semesters of "health class," telling us how to eat, what to eat, how often to exercise, and so on. Okay, I get it. I know that my carrying extra weight is not the healthiest. But those big-ass implants in your chest with foreign material isn't too great for your bod either, I should imagine. I have implants too, so I'm not knocking it; I'm just saying. Or how bout, bitch, you having unprotected sex with multiple partners in your life is not too great for your health. Or, bitch, you running your mouth about my weight—makes me worried for your health. Like, why people criticize? I'll never know that answer.

The answer, of course, to the question is how to deal. Simply, just let it go. Let that person go. Give them a courteous smile (or the middle finger, whatever is your personal style) and seriously never talk to them again.

Weight is one of the most sensitive issues to discuss in this world because everyone is so body-conscious in this day and age. Some may think being too muscular implies that you do steroids. While others think being skinny means that you have an eating disorder. Or people who are larger are not healthy. The truth is that a person's physical size gives little to no indication to any of the above assumptions. Everyone's concern for everyone else's "health" or "looks" is all too much.

I have a dream, and that dream is that one day, we will not not judged based on our measurements or the shapes of our bodies but by our souls and who we are as people and how we treat other people. Could you imagine? No. This concept is far too sophisticated for people to grasp.

So cut that shit out. You don't need any more negativity in your life because, let's face it, you're probably hard enough on yourself. We are all our own worst critics. It's a fact.

Once you cut them out, be sure to challenge yourself to not be a naysayer or judger on someone else's appearance, no matter how bad your day is going. This is one thing I am constantly working on. I've been known to be a gossiper every now and again; it's a nasty habit. So I write on the notes section of my smartphone to look at people as if they were my own flesh and blood. We all were created by God, so if you think about it, everyone is your brother and sister. Just remember that the next time you are going to bash someone for an outfit choice, eating preference, etc. Think about if you would want this said about one of your own family members or even you. Even if you say it behind someone's back, it's still a bad habit, and in the end, it only makes you look insecure.

Cut it all out! Cut the negative people who critique you. Cut your negative thoughts about others. You'll feel better about yourself all the way around, I guarantee. Like, I actually promise you, you will. You might have to make more of a conscious effort at the beginning, but your stock in yourself is going to boom once you take away the "judging a book by it's cover" mentality.

Q: "How do you feel when you see superthin models? Do you ever wish you were like that?"

A: To say, never, would be a lie. I think when I was younger, I'd see models like Kate Moss and envision myself looking like that. I remember watching Michael Jackson's music video for "The Way You Make Me Feel" and thinking that guys would only chase after me if I were as skinny as the girl in that. I was a huge fan of Michael Jackson's, and he was notorious for having the "super thin models" as his love interest. It was heartbreaking. I thought Naomi Campbell in his "In the Closet" video was so sexy and concluded that I would never be sexy unless I was that petite. So, in my younger years, I definitely wished I were a superthin model because that's what my generation and society deemed the epitome of a desirable woman.

Unfortunately, or fortunately, I realized that I will never be that. I could never be that; my structure is not that; I am not tall; I am not lanky; I am not naturally thin. Even when I would go on fad diets and starve myself, at my skinniest, I still had boobs and large hips with thick wrists and ankles. My skeleton is not even a skeleton. My bones and structure are thick; that's the way I was built. Could I have starved myself down to ninety pounds? Probably. But I love food way too much; I always have.

Here's the thing, obviously, by reading this book, you know that I love my curves by now. *Curvy and Loving It*, duh. Sometimes when I see skinny, thin, petite girls, if I feel myself getting any kind of insecurity forming, I think the grass is always greener, meaning that those skinny, thin, petite girls may be wishing they were curvier, that they had a bust, an ass, were shorter, etc. People tend to want what they don't have, and that's fucked up. We need to start wanting what we do have. You'll be happier by desiring what you already posses. To compare yourself to somebody else in general is stupid because you'll never be him or her. On the flip side, he or she will never be you. We only hear negative feedback from outsiders; we rarely hear the envious comments about ourselves. Most people who are jealous, who do not spew hate, will keep it inside. So while you're jealous of someone's flat tummy, remember that they could be jealous of your muscular calves or your full rump. Do you get it?

I'll look at a skinny girl and think, *Oh my, she is gorgeous and breathtaking.* That doesn't take away from me being gorgeous and breathtaking. What I have to offer the world, the opposite sex, myself, my well-being is very different from what a size 0 has to offer. On a superficial level, we both are desirable; it just depends on who you are asking.

Now when I look at superthin models, I admire them for doing what they want to do and looking the way they want to look. Skinny chicks don't have it all that easy in this world anymore either as we are constantly hearing that curvy is in. So I applaud anyone who can put himself or herself out there for the world to judge because they will judge you, honey. Skinny, curvy, malnourished, fat, obese—whatever the world sees you as should have zero effect on the way you view yourself. If you struggle with weight and being too large, too small, too masculine, too whatever, you are living in that body today, and you need to own that body today and love that body today. Work on what you want to fix, but don't beat yourself up over what takes time to change.

I could always be improving on my health, body, and looks, but for the past few years, I can honestly look back at every video I've posted, every picture taken and see myself as beautiful because I was, am, and will be. Inner beauty does radiate to outer beauty, believe it or not. What you feel and what you think and how you treat others will shine. If you're in a bikini and thinking about those superthin models, it's going to reflect. When I'm in a bikini, I imagine myself shooting a Coca Cola ad in the 1950s where girls' roundness was accentuated. I don't throw my arms over my fat rolls, I stick my fat rolls out. It shows not only that am I not hiding anything but that I'm proud of what I've got. Most people will look at that picture and think "what a pretty girl" and not be focusing on your "fat rolls." If they are focusing on your fat rolls, they are dealing with a much deeper internal struggle, and for that you have to keep showing your fat rolls over and over again to show that it's okay to be you in the body you have right now. Thinking about if you're the fattest of your friends in a picture or what your arms look like will show up in your appearance. I can see girls' insecurities not by what they say, dress, or post but by what they don't. What insecure girls say: "Does this look okay?" What confident girls say: "I look amazing." How insecure girls dress: you don't know because you never see an outfit. How confident girls dress: however the fuck they want and let the whole world know about it. What insecure girls post: "I need to lose twenty pounds *now!*" What confident girls post: "Fat and fabulous." You get the point. I mean, it's very possible to be confident without being over the top or narcissistic, but if you're not quite at the confident and silent scale yet, be confident and loud—it'll help. It'll be like you're screaming at yourself that you're good enough.

Superthin models are gorgeous, but that's not me. I would never wish to be anyone but me—too much time, energy, and pain it takes to try and be someone else. It's like a race that you'll never finish, and in the end, you'll just be exhausted and worn out. Save that energy for you and put it into something you can achieve. Your body right now is wonderful; it's allowing you to breathe, walk, talk, read, etc. So once you love that body, that energy can be spent into things your body and you want to do: write a book, go on a vacation, go running, start a cooking blog, become a mermaid for a day, swim with the dolphins, eat the cupcakes, buy the shoes, go back to school, have a baby, do it all! This goes for you, too, superthin models. You were what I wished to be when I was a little girl, so don't go being insecure now.

Q: "Do people make fun of your weight/how you dress?"

A: On a daily basis. Ever since I've gained popularity on the Internet, I would say that people make fun of my weight over one hundred times a day. This includes comments on all my videos, social media, gossip sites, and so on. I can never be on a television show without reviewers talking about my body. In the past three years, I can't recall one television appearance where something about my weight has not been said. This includes after the fact. When I was on *America's Got Talent*, Howard Stern danced with me on stage and was super sweet and wonderful. The next day on his radio show he compared me to Pamela Anderson if I were to lose twenty pounds, to which he corrected and said, "Forty pounds." This was heartbreaking to hear from someone I idolized. However, it didn't change the fact that I thought, nay, knew, that I looked hot on AGT. Sometimes I watch this one clip of me online from my episode, and the thumbnail in that hot-pink dress, currently has over sixty million views. Half the comments are how fat and disgusting I look; the other half are telling me they want to bang me, date me, love me, or they are begging me to do porn. So there you have it: my weight comments in a nutshell. Literally go to any single one of my videos, and you will find a debate on whether I'm fat or not.

How I dress sort of goes hand in hand with that, and I have gotten ridiculed for my personal style for just as long. When it comes to how I dress, I find my confidence in movie characters like Romy and Michelle from *Romy and Michelle's High School Reunion*. These girls got made fun of all the time in high school for they way they dressed, but they were happy, and that's what spoke to me. They stayed true to their style because that's what they liked, and they were able to flourish by being themselves. Wear what you like because it's your money and your body that you are dressing. If you want to follow the trends and keep with what's cool, do that because it will make you feel more confident. I love it; I support it 100 percent. If you want to wear a tutu, wear a tutu. If anything makes you feel uncomfortable, don't wear it. I can't tell you how many times I've put on tight dresses and taken them off because I felt stuffed in them. Other times, I've put on a dress three times too small for me (i.e., *America's Got Talent*) and felt like a million bucks. It all depends on the day/time/mood for me. Clothes are easy to change, and they are the most stupid thing to judge someone for. They are wearing those clothes for a reason. You can put me in a Chanel white blazer and Seven jeans, but I'm still going to be the same obnoxious Trish I would be in a neon-pink spandex minidress I got at a stripper store on Hollywood Blvd. The way we dress is an expression of who we are and what we feel. Others may choose to wear outfits based on what is acceptable by society in order not to stand out too much. I don't discourage that mentality either. I understand that we are all not flamingos that want to splash in the water for attention, and that's what makes this world go 'round. A girl who wears the same Abercrombie denim shorts as everyone else is simply framing the main attraction, which is her. She chose a simple frame, and that's beautiful. I choose a frame made out of trash, but it still doesn't change the picture that it's showcasing.

To get "made fun of" is such a childish thing to me. I am a grown-ass woman who doesn't give a single fuck if you want to snicker, laugh, or stare at me. The beauty about getting older is that you really don't give any fucks about what people think about you. When you get older, you have more important things to worry about then if a skirt is too short or a shirt is too sloppy. I get up and wear what I want. I've worn Halloween costumes as dresses to parties, and I've worn boxer shorts to the grocery store. I've worn my Christian Louboutin heels to the gym, and I've worn Birkenstock sandals into SAKS. Who cares? Really, who cares? I'll tell you who cares: people with no lives. And don't you dare sink down to that level. Anyone who tries to bring you down is very clearly already underneath you or below you. Stay on top. Rise above. If you go down to their level, it's a really bad angle for your chin.

Q: **"What is your perfect weight?"**

A: It doesn't exist. A perfect weight does not exist. I use to always say 130. I've been to 130, and I think that my face is too gaunt. I said, okay, maybe 140. At 140, my gut is too prominent. I visualize me at one hundred pounds and think how flat my ass would look. I go up and down more than Oprah Winfrey herself on the scale. I've seen my body and face change drastically while staying the exact same weight. Your body, face, and muscles are always evolving. Lately, a lot of people have been saying that it looks like I lost weight in my videos. It's because I'm maturing; so naturally, I'm losing baby fat off my face. When people see me in pictures, they think I gained weight because my body is still round or my hips are fuller. Within the past year, my hips have gained two inches while maintaining the exact same weight I was in 2012. You can't decide where you want to lose and where you want to gain. Even if you get surgery to fix or enhance your body, age will change your look, whether you want it or not. Medications from those procedures can change your water retention or the mechanics of your body and the skin texture. Your environment and your situations will alter your appearance. This is all fact and all something that is ultimately out of your control until you can manage it. Even when you manage it, you still can't stop the hands of time or the surprises from Mother Nature.

I know so many people that once they hit their "goal weight" are unhappy. Why? Because they were expecting something else. This is why I don't place goals on my body or weight because it sets me up for disappointment. Instead, I work on molding my body and tweaking what I can, working on areas for improvement, rather than just aiming for "the perfect weight."

What's my perfect weight? 180. That is what I am right now, and I am happy. If you were to ask me this time last year, my perfect weight was two hundred. I was happy. If you ask me in a couple months, my answer will surely be different; I will guarantee that. My perfect weight is the weight I am when I am happy.

Q:
"What is the one thing you love most about yourself?"

A: Oh how could I possibly pick just one thing? Please—I just wrote an entire book on how wonderful I am and how to be as wonderful as me. I love that I don't apologize for being me. I love that I look so smoking hot in lingerie. I love that I'm kind to my family. I love that my heart is so big and open, even though it's been smashed to pieces over and over again. I love that I don't let life jade me. I love that I can see the good in everyone, even those who are mean to me. I love that I can see the beauty in everyone, even in those who don't see it in themselves. I love that I eat whatever I want. I love that I struggle with that love. I love that I have been able to achieve every life goal I've ever had (I had to make a new list to not get bored). I love that I can meet anyone I set out to meet. I love that I don't get distracted by people who tell me I can't. I love that I get distracted by love. I love the fact that I love love. I love the way that I look at myself in a mirror. I love that I take amazing selfies. I love that I live to love God. I love my boobs; they are amazing—thank you, saline. I love my butt because it's so cushy and never gets hurt. I love my eyes; my eyes are the most gorgeous blue you'll ever see. I love my obsession for pink. I love knowing everything pop culture. I love that I hum to myself. I love talking to myself when no one's around. I love my voice and how it cracks each note at the perfectly imperfect pitch. I love the way I talk. I love the way I walk. I love that my body wobbles when it tries to run. I love how great I style my hair. I love how I talk fast. I love that I read fast. I love that I spit when I get excited. I love my huge bladder and being able to hold a pee all the way to Vegas. I love how I can make other people smile. I love that when I cry, I look like a mutant. I love my little sausage toes. I love my midget feet. I love my warm thighs. I love that I can pretend I'm other people. I love the touch of my own skin. I love the softness of my waist. I love the weight of my own arms. I love the heaviness of my hair. I love that I laugh so hard, I squeak. I love my nostrils that flare when I'm excited. I love all the excess hair on my lips so I can wax it off each month. I love that I'm twisted. I love that people think I'm insane. I love not being normal. I love not fitting in. I love fitting in. I love the attention I get. I love the attention my boobs get. I love smiling. I love laughing. I love praying. I love getting out of bed and brushing my teeth. I love that nothing matches on my body, hair, or apartment. I love that I can love myself. I love that I can say all the things I love about myself.

I mean, I could go on. Who wants a sequel to this book?

Q: "What is one thing you could go back and tell your younger you regarding appearance?"

A: The one thing I wish I would've told young Trish was how beautiful she was. Like, I look at young Trish, and I see a girl full of pain from torment and abuse of people making fun of her weight, her clothes, her eyebrows, her hair, chest, eyes, legs, hair on body parts, just so much cruelness, when, in reality, as an outsider, I see a really stunning girl. You may not think you're not skinny enough, pretty enough, and be in your oh-one-day-when-I'm-older-I'll-look like-her phase, but you are so beautiful right now that you can't even see it. It's so sad. Girls will tweet me saying how they know they're fat, but I help them get through. Most of these girls are half the size I was at their age; they don't even know fat. Our minds are so warped of our own selves, especially in your teenage years. It breaks my heart. So when girls say they are getting made fun of, I get pics of some of these girls who said they thought about taking their own lives because they're not pretty enough and yet they are physically gorgeous and I'm sure great people inside as well. Like, this one girl looked like a young Brooke Shields to me, and she said she doesn't want to live because of her looks. I wrote back to her a letter almost as long as this book and said that she needs to model; she needs to show the world outside of her small town her beauty because she literally was one of the prettiest young girls I had ever seen. My stomach hurt so bad that so many of these young girls couldn't see that—teenage Trish included.

I'll post pictures on my social media from when I was in school, and even though I get hate on every single one of my photos, those never do. Even the ones trying to be mean will say, "Trish, you were so pretty back then, what happened?" Go figure, huh? I truly was an attractive girl, but I never felt more disgusting than I did in my junior high years. I entered a beauty pageant in the eighth grade and travelled two hours outside of my home town for it. It was in a suburb right outside Chicago; over three hundred girls from all over Illinois entered. I placed in the top ten, and I think that's when I was able to start seeing myself as beautiful. Isn't that ironic? Isn't that crazy, in a sense? I had to travel outside my town, seek approval from strangers just to start sort-of kind-of believing I could be...maybe...attractive. Even looking back at pictures of me in my early adult life, I remember being told how fat I was or thinking that I was obese. Looking back now, I was so fit. What was I thinking? I was thinking what the world wanted me to think. I was thinking what my neurotic, middle-aged managers wanted me to think. It was such bullshit. I really wish I could go back to young Trish throughout all stages of my life and just shake her and say, "Wake up! You are beautiful, stop wasting this time worrying about a problem that literally does not exist."

Chances are, you are more attractive than you know too. So maybe I can't go back and tell my younger self all this, but I'm telling you. You can be the young Trish. I'm telling you to stop worrying about your weight. If you have baby fat, you'll outgrow it. If you're meant to get on a fit path, you'll find it when the time is right. If you are too skinny and want curves, puberty doesn't hit everyone at the same time, and womanhood has nothing to do with how big your boobs can grow. There is something so special and unique about you that I guarantee you either see as a flaw or can't see at all. Sometimes our biggest "flaws" are what make us that unique and true beauty that not everyone can hold. Look at Tyra and her big forehead or me and my wide-set eyes that people would call me "downs" or "alien" for. I believe these features not only have us stand apart from the rest but actually add something to our look that make people think, "What is it about that girl?" I promise you, you have that too. You may not have discovered it yet, but you will, and you will be so thankful and blessed for it.

I also want to tell you young girls: life isn't about pretty. Pretty fades. True beauty will shine forever. I want you to stay focused. I want you to stay motivated. Whether you're the most popular girl in school or the freaky girl who eats lunch alone in the bathroom, keep your eyes on the prize. High school and even college is such a short little blip on the large scale of life. The people you are with now do not define you. You must stay hungry and go after your dreams beyond what you're living now. Think bigger; dream bigger. Dream so big that people call you crazy for dreaming such things. I may be insane, but I'm also brilliant, so listen to me. I've been called crazy so many times for thinking that I could make a career out of entertainment. Well, I have; I am; and I am doing it. I literally created my own job out of thin air. That goes to show that anything is possible. Don't ever self-doubt either. Maybe you are not technically the best at something or your credentials don't trump another's, but your different approach to what you do in life could be the very brilliant thing this world needs to evolve, change, grow, learn, and succeed.

Q: "What is your biggest secret to being confident?"

A: And here it all comes down to this. *Being confident means being you.* It's that simple. Be you and accept it. Be you and love it. Be you and flaunt it. Be you and work it. You need to just be yourself and not let the outside world change you. If you can be strong, be different, be true, you're being you. It's so simple, isn't it? Don't let outside forces change you; you change those outside forces. Don't let the world change you; you need to change the world. It all starts and ends with you. You can be happy if you just be you. Why do we find it so difficult to be ourselves? It can be vulnerable to be the bare you, but it's also very liberating. If people think I'm fake, superficial, or any other meaningless adjective, that is not my problem because I can only be me. I never understood how a person could be "fake" anyway. Are we not all humans with blood and oxygen and breath and life? That seems pretty real to me.

I want you to get all that you can out of this life, and I want you to enjoy it for everything it has to offer. Give what you can, and receive what you get. Don't deny compliments. Don't be afraid to take chances. Don't be afraid of failing. Don't be afraid to expose who you are, no matter how scary it may seem.

The world has seven billion people in it but there is not one, single, other you. You are it. You represent you, and you can change the world. Literally, one person can. You can change other's lives. You have the power. When you are just *you*, others have to respect that. When you are you, you're going to radiate so much light and love into this world. When you are you, you will be able to walk into any room, any situation, and never worry about anything. Being you is so freeing, and it's so very simple. Just let all your inhibitions go. Wake up every day and say, "Yay! I'm me." I cannot tell you how proud I am of myself. I cannot tell you how much I enjoy my own company. I cannot tell you how much I want to share myself with others because I know the love that I have for me and the love I have for humanity. I am me, and you are you and in this world. We are creating something amazing just by that simple mantra. We are enough as is. You are good enough right now. You will be fine. Even with everything you've gone through in life, you are still here, and that is because of you. This life is all about you. This time is yours. Nothing can hold you back. Nothing will hold you back–as long as you are you.

Be happy. Be confident. Be you.

Manufactured by Amazon.ca
Bolton, ON

35310108R00063